What to Say—and What *Not* to Say

A GUIDE TO HELP YOU
CARE FOR OTHERS

HELPING
THOSE IN
GRIEF

H. NORMAN
WRIGHT

Regal

From Gospel Light
Ventura, California, U.S.A.

Published by Regal
From Gospel Light
Ventura, California, U.S.A.
www.regalbooks.com
Printed in the U.S.A.

Library of Congress Cataloging-in-Publication Data
Wright, H. Norman.
Helping those in grief / H. Norman Wright.
p. cm.
ISBN 978-0-8307-5871-5 (hard cover)
ISBN 978-0-8307-6215-6 (trade paper)
1. Church work with the bereaved. 2. Bereavement—Religious aspects—Christianity.
I. Title.
BV4330.W75 2011
259'.6—dc22
2011011728

Rights for publishing this book outside the U.S.A. or in non-English languages are
administered by Gospel Light Worldwide, an international not-for-profit ministry.
For additional information, please visit www.glww.org, email info@glww.org, or write to
Gospel Light Worldwide, 1957 Eastman Avenue, Ventura, CA 93003, U.S.A.

To order copies of this book and other Regal products in bulk quantities,
please contact us at 1-800-446-7735.

Contents

Shattered Dreams

The Beginning of a Journey of Grief

I was standing on a field watching the participants of a cancer survivors Relay for Life gathering. One of the survivors marching around the field was my wife, Joyce. As I watched, my cell phone went off, and I saw that it was a close friend I had known for almost 40 years. His first words were, "My son Matt is in heaven." I wasn't sure I had heard him right. "What? What did you say?" was my response. He replied again with the same words: "Matt is in heaven."

I felt stunned. Shocked. Not fully comprehending or believing what I had heard. No death notification is easy to accept, but especially not this one—a vibrant and quality 23-year-old young man with his sights set on graduate school, and planning to marry in two months' time.

I'd known him since he was born, had taken him fishing and had long conversations with him. I waited until after the Relay for Life event was over to share the news with anyone else.

A few weeks later, I flew back to the Midwest to be with my friend. On my trip back, I wrote my reflections on the experience and called it "Shattered Dreams." Here is what I wrote:

It is through our dreams that meaning as well as delight are brought into our life. Meaning and delight are closely aligned with a sense of hope of something yet to come—something on the horizon that is better and fulfilling, bringing a greater sense of meaning to our life. Some dreams, however, not only go unfulfilled or are altered, but they also are shattered and destroyed, and with them a portion of our life as well.

I saw this in the eyes and posture of this young man's father and in his siblings, in his fiancée and her family, in his grandparents and friends. Many times I heard this phrase or something similar expressed: "There's an empty place in my life, an immense hole, and it will never be filled in again."

I listened to stories of this young man who was on the verge of graduating from college and moving into marriage. From those who loved and accepted him for who he was I heard about his triumphs and his dreams, his struggles and his battles. There was no idealization of him, only an honest sense of love and acceptance. His photographs showed that infectious smile, and his greeting seemed to leap out: "Hey, Norm, how's it going?" It felt strange to look at a recent family photo of him with his father, mother, brothers and fiancée. I began to see the portrait with two faces missing, his and his fiancée's. The family appeared to have shrunk right in front of my eyes.

And then there was the fiancée, a young woman on the verge of a new life, but on whom grief had settled like a shroud. Her entire life was in upheaval as though an earthquake had destroyed her personal landscape. It was total destruction as her graduation came the day following his death, and her birthday the next day; in just a few weeks would have been her wedding. For the first time in four-and-a-half years, she was alone, no longer in a relationship with her future husband. She was literally pushed into being single again, with no warning or preparation.

Not only did she lose her love, but she also lost the experience of becoming a member of his family and the blending of her family with his. These two families would never have children, grandchildren or cousins together. She would be faced with significant times that were sure to reactivate her grief: graduations, birthdays, the wedding date, going on to graduate school without him. She had brought out the best in him, and he the best in her. Each was already considered a member of the other's family.

In the future, whichever man fell in love with her and wanted to marry her would need to be *very* special, for her first fiancé was unique. He was a communicator; he was vulnerable; he shared feelings; and he was adventuresome. This future event would not only be an adjustment for her, but for siblings and parents as well. Unfortunately, any man would probably be looked at very carefully and compared with her lost love.

The future for anyone close to him and her and to their families, as well as others not even involved, now was, and would be, impacted by this loss.

This is what a sudden tragic death does. It cuts you adrift with no compass or steering mechanism. There is not only the fear of becoming lost but also of being forgotten over time. For many in her situation, this would be the case, but not with her, for she is too greatly loved by his family, and she will always be part of his family. But a fiancé(e) and his or her family members run the risk of becoming forgotten grievers. It's imperative that we who are called to minister to those in grief be sensitive to those who may be overlooked and fall through the cracks.

The youngest brother could fall into this category. When you're 17, and trying to navigate the waters of adolescence—figuring out who you are and where you are going, and handling two years of a mother's death-threatening disease of pancreatic cancer—how do you handle the death of your 23-year-old brother, who had been drawing closer to you during the past year? It's so easy to turn inward and only carry on conversations with yourself about these issues.

And his aunt could easily be forgotten. The dinner we had with her (with homemade coconut pie) was a delight. She is an amazing, energetic woman who, at a young age, contracted polio and now deals with the post-polio syndrome. Confined to a motorized cart, she does everything she possibly can. But her words of loss still echo in my mind: "Everywhere I turn I'm reminded of him. Everywhere, I see something he helped me with at home. He was so patient and helpful, whether it was about a light bulb, the lawn, my driveway, my car, a cabinet door. My helper is gone." Not only has she lost a nephew as close to her as her own son, but she now has a multitude of secondary losses as well.

His mom was staying at her mother's place during this time, getting some rest and waiting to have her stomach drained again because of her cancer. The depth of her grief is probably immeasurable.

What did I do while I was there? I was *there*. I was present to be or do whatever was needed. I baked chocolate chip cookies for the staff and family each day, which evaporated in a feeding frenzy. Listening to, interacting with and following the lead of others filled hours. And we laughed and cried. These are two of God's gifts that make up the grieving process. It's so refreshing to be in an environment where emotions can be so freely expressed.

Arkansas at this time of year is lush, with the variations of every green found in the color wheel. This was especially evident as we drove across the pastures and farmland to where he was killed. We stopped the truck and began to walk on a path into the dense forest. Eventually, we came to the location. His dad, brother and two others had erected a cross and a monument of boulders upon the spot where he had died. A line of rocks outlined where his body had lain.

His dad knelt in silence and gently patted the area where his head had rested upon the ground. His older brother had rubbed some of his blood upon the horizontal arm of the cross, and though faint it was still visible. We stood in silence for a while listening to the sounds of rain hitting the canopy of leaves blocking out the sky above us, and then we had a time of prayer. We walked through the foliage to a small meandering stream, hoping to avoid ticks (which we didn't), and selected a few rocks to bring back to help brace the cross. This was a special, almost sacred, occasion that I will never forget. We spent hours talking, reminiscing and reflecting. On several occasions his dad would lead in prayer. We talked about death and life and the Lord, and the future.

His father shared that he didn't want to just get through this grief. He wanted it to cause him to be a better man, a better father and husband, to love better, to have a more significant impact upon others. The present is a time of constant pain that ebbs back and forth in its intensity, bringing agony and tears. But it is being faced directly. I just wish every family would embrace their losses and grief as this family has. This tragedy cuts deeply but will not be wasted.

I went to be with my friends to comfort, help, minister and grieve with them. But I return having been ministered to as well as changed by their faith and prayer life, for my friend is indeed a man of prayer who touches everyone's life.

All of our lives have been changed; and in time, with God's presence and grace, it will all be to His glory. Death and the grave and Satan do not triumph, but God's kingdom will.

We are not in charge of our own timetable, nor do we understand or need to understand the timing. It's just that Matt got to the banquet table sooner than expected. But just wait . . . someday we'll be joining you. Hallelujah! "I am the resurrection and the life. He who believes in me will live, even though he dies" (John 11:25).

The day after returning home, I did what his dad and younger brother do several times a day. They call his phone to hear his voice and greeting once again. "Hey, what's going on? This is Matt." It was good to hear his voice once again.

I wrote these reflections during the flight home to Bakersfield, California. My wife wouldn't be home when I arrived; friends had taken her to Cedar's Sinai Hospital in Los Angeles for a physical in preparation for her brain surgery the next week. And so, we, too, were entering the valley of uncertainty and waiting upon the Lord for His direction, grace and guidance. He is our certainty in uncertain times.

For the joy of the LORD is your strength (Neh. 8:10).

He will be the stability of your times (Isa. 33:6, *ESV*).

Postscript: Just about a month later, Matt's mother lost her three-year battle with pancreatic cancer; and two months after that, my wife lost her four-year battle with her brain tumors. The valley of grief was now filled with many others.

Personal Questions for a Grief Counselor

Throughout this book you will encounter many stories, some of which may hit very close to home. The stories may even bring up some of your own losses and grief. To increase your awareness of your own experiences with death and the ways in which your attitudes have been influenced, consider the following questions:

1. What was your first encounter with death? Try to recall your feelings and needs at that time. How did others respond to your feelings and needs? What is your most vivid image associated with that first loss experience?

2. How was the topic of death dealt with in your family? (Was it ignored? Considered taboo? Openly and matter-of-factly discussed?)

3. Can you remember the first funeral you attended? How were you prepared for this experience? What do you remember about it? What feelings did you have? How was the funeral and your response influenced by religion and culture?

4. What significant losses have you had throughout your life? Which one was the most painful, and why? In what ways has it affected your life? In what ways, if any, has it affected the way you do therapy?[1]

Before you turn the page, take the time to answer these questions as best you can. Understanding your own issues with loss and death is one of the necessary steps to becoming more capable of walking with others in their grief journey. In addition, it is important that you have completed reading *The Complete Guide to Counseling* prior to using this resource, as *Helping Those in Grief* builds upon that book, and I will refer to it on numerous occasions.

1

One Stitch at a Time

To introduce you to the world of grief counseling, the following first-person account relates a husband's ongoing journey as he grieves the death of his wife. These are the thoughts of a real man going through real grief. His comment of asking God to heal his heart "one stitch at a time" is so true of the slow process of grief. There are no quick fixes.

What you read here is very similar to what you will hear other people say as you counsel them through their grief. Think about what you would say to this man and how you would minister to him.

I suppose I was not much different from most men when it came to dealing with death, whether it was my own death or that of a loved one. I would not allow myself to fully contemplate my own death, and most certainly not that of my wife, Susan, whom I loved and was devoted to for more than 20 years. Yet, in the span of three short months, Susan died from complications associated with breast cancer.

To say that I was unprepared for her sudden death would be a gross understatement. I was totally and completely caught off guard, mentally and spiritually. As a result, I was thrown into a mental and physical tailspin of denial and disbelief, a denial that manifested in an overwhelming sense of guilt and depression and a state of mourning that was beyond psychological comprehension.

I suddenly found myself trying to deal with a situation that just a few days before was beyond the scope of my daily life, much less a soon-to-be reality. I found myself grasping for reasons why this would happen to Susan, how it could happen so suddenly and what was to happen to me. Without warning the ebb and flow of what was once a normal and happy life had drastically changed for the worst. All that I knew and loved had not only changed but was lost forever. A wave of deep depression and extreme selfishness washed over my soul with the loss of Susan.

I had what I considered a perfect marriage relationship. I was a kept man in every sense of the word. That is to say whatever my need, Susan willingly and happily met that need. Whether it was sexually, socially, physically or spiritually, she was there. Susan was not just my wife; she was my best friend, closest confidant and a voice of sound reason when I was unreasonable. I suddenly found myself having to deal with life in all of its fullness, feeling both alone and abandoned. I felt as if I was on an island of humanity, isolated within myself, void of family and friends. For the first time in my married life, I had no answers for what lay before me or what I was about to endure. I found myself an unwilling participant in a mental endurance run with no end in sight. All I knew was that I needed help to navigate this run, and I needed it now.

Isolated, depressed and feeling sorry for myself, I realized I needed help that was beyond my spiritual, physical and mental abilities. So I turned to the roots of my raising—a raising that required a rededication of my life to church and, most importantly, a closer walk with Jesus. Yet, I was conflicted on the best way to accomplish this; for after all, in recent years, I was not actively participating in church. This made me feel somewhat guilty asking my church for help, but I was desperate and I was willing to do anything and seek any advice if it would ease my pain, isolation and depression. As it happened, my pastor informed me of a class that was being conducted by another local church, called "GriefShare."

Unable to function in daily life, I found myself operating on autopilot. However, I was able to pull myself together enough to contact the church conducting the GriefShare class and make arrangements to attend the next available class. As it turned out, attending the GriefShare class was one of the best decisions I made in the early stages of my grief and mourning. I found that the class, while informal, was as its name implied, shared grief. It was not a course in which, after a class or two, you would be apathetic. The class was not designed for that; however it was a class that brought together others who were grieving as deeply as I was, although for different reasons, while creating a common bond. Additionally, it provided me with an outlet and a facility to freely express my feelings with others who were enduring similar circumstances of grief and mourning.

In the early stages of the class, I noticed that a phrase kept popping up throughout the 13-week course. As I attended more classes, I came to cringe at its utterance. The phrase was "starting a new normal." I didn't know what it meant, nor could anyone fully explain or define what that phrase was supposed to mean. As it turned out, the phrase had a different meaning for each person. My challenge was to discover what my "new normal" was to be.

While I truly can't say that I have discovered its complete meaning as it applies to me, I do believe that I'm beginning to understand its meaning a little better. As I take stock of my life, as it is now, I realize that my life is a circle from sunrise to sundown. As long as it continues in this manner, I know that I will always have a new day dawning. I believe that eventually my circled life of sunrise and sundown will straighten into a path laden with peril but also a new beginning. When that day comes, then I'll be able to say that I do have a "new normal" that begins today.

The *New International Version* of the Bible states in Ecclesiastes 7:2, "It is better to go to a house of mourning than to go to a house of feasting, for death is the destiny of every man." I found this passage while searching for some divine or profound meaning to my life as it is now. As I dwelt on its concept, I did struggle with its meaning as I understood it. While death is the destiny of every man, it is inescapable, just as mourning is. However, the house of feasting is just a temporary condition. The feeling of euphoria, while wondrous, is short-lived and provides little comfort or spiritual assistance. The house of mourning, on the other hand, is a time-tested tempering of your soul and spirit, and faith that your prayers will be answered. Mourning, however painful, is God's way to test your faith, and the trying of your faith by divine fires. Once completed, you will have faith that you will stand the test of time and your devotion to God's plan for you.

Through these past few months, I prayed many prayers and there were many prayers prayed on my behalf by family and friends. However, none of them seemed to have reached the ear of God. Then, one day when I was in my hour of deepest depression and isolation, I began to pray a very simple prayer.

Lord, You know my needs. All I ask is that You provide a single healing stitch to my heart once a day. I know that over time, while the scar in my heart will always remain, the healing can begin.

I find that I miss Susan more than I can say, and I will forever love her. I know that the healing process of my heart has begun, however gradual, for God does answer prayer if you only have faith.[1]

The focus of the rest of this book—helping people navigate through their grief and move toward recovery—is one of the most critical areas of need and ministry. The rest of the chapters in this book are interactive, giving you the opportunity to consider numerous real case studies to see how you would counsel the people described in each study. At the end of each chapter, I provide not only the approach to counseling I would use with the people in the case studies, but also the actual wording that would be most helpful in each situation. As well, I mention some grief resources of my own, but many others that I have found helpful as I work with those in grief.

As you seek to expand or improve the way you help others in this critical area of ministry, may you always rely upon the strength and wisdom of the Lord to minister to those who are grieving the loss of a loved one.

2

Case Studies
What Would You Say or Do?

Loss and grief are a constant in the life of every church congregation and every neighborhood. Where you live and where you worship may provide you, or has provided you, a multitude and variety of situations in which you will be called on to counsel and coach those who are dealing with grief as the natural result of the death of a family member or friend.

Whether you are a lay counselor or a professional counselor, there will be times when you would like some guidance as you sort through the issues surrounding grief. *Helping Those in Grief* has been designed to increase knowledge and growth in this area of counseling. In addition to being informative and educational, it is also challenging and interactive. You will read about grief and death, but you will also have the opportunity to interact with actual counseling cases and determine how you would respond. Upon completion of your reading the entire text, you may want to revisit these counseling cases and further apply what you have learned.

Case Studies

The following are cases from my own experience. I present the facts of each case briefly, and then ask you to respond to several questions before proceeding to the next case. If you are using this book as a text in any type of course, it would be helpful to engage in small-group discussion of the various questions. At the conclusion of this chapter, I will give my responses to these questions. At the conclusion of each of the other chapters there will be an additional case study or actual verbatim counseling session so that you can apply what you have been reading.

CASE 1

The parents and three siblings of a 23-year-old woman come in for grief counseling. All are neat in appearance—well dressed and fairly quiet. The parents are first to speak about their daughter. They begin with a description that characterizes her as a quality young woman—their first-born. She was gifted in every area of her life and had a bright future ahead of her. The parents go into great detail about her abilities and accomplishments, stopping every now and then because of their inability to talk. Often all five family members are in tears. Two weeks prior to this meeting, the daughter, carrying her seven-month-old unborn child, and her mother-in-law, were driving on a freeway when a truck struck and killed all of them. Since that time, every member of this family has been struggling.

QUESTIONS

1. How would you begin this counseling session? Describe your exact words.
2. What would be your goal in this initial session?
3. What would you say or ask to engage the three siblings?
4. What would you want the entire family to take away from this session in a tangible way?
5. Based on the information in the case study description, identify all the possible grievers.
6. What are the factors that contribute to this loss being a complicated grieving process?

CASE 2

A seven-year-old child called the 911 dispatchers. Her words were articulate and quite knowledgeable. She lived with her mother, who had passed out on the floor. The little girl described the symptoms and then said her mother wasn't breathing. The dispatcher heard the little girl go over and check the mother's pulse and then, over the phone, heard the little girl give her CPR. Unfortunately, the mother died. The phone line was kept open, and the dispatcher heard the sheriff's deputy arrive and then pick up the little girl and hold her and talk to her for 25 minutes.

You have been called because your name and number were found on the kitchen counter. When you arrive, the sheriff brings the little girl, whom you've never met before, over to you.

QUESTIONS

1. Describe how you would introduce yourself to this child.
2. Describe what you believe this child has experienced.
3. What information do you need at this time?
4. What is your goal in working with this child?
5. What questions might you ask? What questions might the child be wondering but *not* asking? How would you bring these questions to the surface as well as answer them?

CASE 3

I was at dinner with a close friend after an intense day in a graduate class on grief and trauma. Five minutes into the conversation, he casually mentioned, "By the way, Norm, my wife's former father-in-law committed suicide yesterday." The father-in-law had given an indication of wanting to do this for two years, but no one took him seriously. His wife's twin children by her previous marriage have experienced five major death losses in the last five years—their own father, an aunt, an uncle, a grandmother and now a grandfather. They were 16 when the first death occurred. What do they need, and how do you help them? They've made an appointment to see you this week.

QUESTIONS

1. Describe your initial comments and questions.
2. Which of the losses do you address first, and how would you accomplish this?
3. Is it best to see them together or separately? Why?
4. What do you think some of their questions and concerns might be at this time?
5. What information would you need to help them move forward in their lives?

CASE 4

A man in his fifties has made an appointment for what he describes as a "complicated" grief case. He is supposed to testify in his son's murder case. In fact, both the prosecution and the defense have subpoenaed him. The murder victim was his daughter. Thus, in addition to the intense loss (of both children), he feels conflicted and torn.

QUESTIONS

1. What are the feelings that might be involved in this situation?
2. What are some of the questions you would ask this man at this time?
3. What type of ongoing support could be created for him?
4. Describe the various types of losses he is experiencing.
5. Describe how you would help him grieve.

CASE 5

In the initial session, a 30-year-old woman shares that her husband was killed in a truck accident five years ago after they had been married for only 14 months. Together, they had two young children. The man she has been with for the five years since her first husband's death died two months ago as a suicide. She had come home with one of her children, and they found that he had hanged himself. She has two children by him. Now she has four children under the age of seven to raise.

QUESTIONS

1. Describe the type of grief you may encounter in this case.
2. Identify the various losses that have occurred in this woman's life.
3. Other than grief counseling, what else might you need to do in order to help her?
4. Describe the possible trauma symptoms she may be experiencing.
5. What resources would you recommend for her, and how should they be used?

CASE 6

A woman in her fifties describes the time when she lost her child who was born three months prematurely. The baby lived for only 12 days. She said, "At least with this child, I know why she died." At that time, she had one small son. In a few years, she had another son and daughter.

Years later, her 21-year-old son committed suicide. He was described as a compliant, happy, easygoing boy. Following his death, her husband came home one day sobbing, which continued for some time. He said he had seen a vision of the Lord holding a child.

More recently, her 25-year-old son, who had already served time in prison, was shot while running from a property where he was trying to steal some items. He was shot at least 12 times by the owner. The case is pending with the DA at this time.

This struggling mother is just now considering getting some help. She also struggles with what others have told her. Her mother and others have said that she's under a generational curse. She shared that she has lost who she is because of what her son did.

QUESTIONS

1. Describe what you would attempt to discover and accomplish in your initial session together.
2. Describe the possible complications of this woman's grief.
3. How would you discover her coping skills?
4. Describe the support system you would recommend for this family.

CASE 7

A woman comes for counseling after the loss of her husband. She has a very distant relationship with his family. His parents did not want a funeral or graveside service, but instead wanted a resurrection service. They believed they could resurrect their son from the dead. After the graveside service, the mother of the man kept praying and walking around the grave, trying to resurrect her son, until the mortuary workers asked her to leave so they could complete the burial. This wife is coming to see you about her loss as well as about how to handle her husband's relatives who have now become very intrusive.

QUESTIONS

1. Is it best to respond first to her grief or to the problem of the in-laws who are creating more pain for her? Why?
2. Family dysfunction intensifies at the time of death. Just from the sparse information given in this case, what is your analysis of this situation?

3. What could this grieving woman do to handle her deceased husband's relatives?
4. What could you do to ensure that she will follow through on the suggestions and guidelines that the two of you have worked out?

CASE 8

A woman was called by the police department and asked to return home after neighbors had called them because of smoke coming from the garage. When they went into the garage, they found some smoldering material and that her 37-year-old husband had died of a heart attack. The children were upset, and the police suggested that she tell them their father had gone to heaven. She said she couldn't do that because they were Seventh-Day Adventists. They didn't believe a person's soul went straight to heaven; they believed in soul sleep.

QUESTIONS

1. Describe what you think would be the emotional state of this mother and her children.
2. The mother asks you, "How am I going to survive? He was all I had, and I can't work because I have lupus and fibromyalgia."
3. She also asks you, "Do you believe in heaven? How soon does a person go there when he or she dies?"

Case Study Responses

The following section contains the kind of responses I made or would make to the questions posed in the eight case studies. Before reading further, you might want to return to each case summary and read the questions again to get reacquainted with the issues.

CASE 1

This is about family counseling—parents and siblings—after the auto accident death of their 23-year-old daughter who was carrying a seven-month-old unborn baby. They were riding in a car with the girl's mother-in-law, who also died:

1. After greeting each person, I would validate the fact that they have experienced a great loss. If I didn't know already, I would ask the name of the daughter, as well as her mother-in-law's, and whenever I made reference to either person, I would use her name rather than refer to either person in a general way. One of the first questions I ask is, "Tell me about _____ [the daughter]," and then I ask each member of the family to respond. Too often, children are left out of the interaction. After each person has responded, my next question is, "Would you describe for me what the last two weeks have been like?" so that each family member has a chance to tell his or her story. Within that question, I often ask how each person heard the news and to describe his or her reaction.

2. My goal is to have each person tell his or her story, normalize for them what they are experiencing, and then educate them about grief and what to expect in the future (using the handout in chapter 3 titled "Crazy Feelings of Grief"). I'd also want to find out about their support system as well as give some suggestions to eliminate pressure from other individuals. I also mention that each of them may grieve in a different way and with a different intensity. That's all right, and it's not a sign that the person whose grief is less intense doesn't care. I ask each person, "How can your other family members support you at this time?"

3. Some of the questions directed toward the parents could be asked of the siblings. I also let everyone know that I would be willing to meet with each one individually. One reason for this is that the deceased was described as a "special, gifted" individual; but was she in the eyes

of the siblings? Sometimes, even in the initial session, I ask for a favorite memory from siblings. Some may have a mixture of feelings. At some point, I would ask the parents and siblings alike if there was any unfinished business or any issues between them and the deceased, or if there was something they wished they could have said to her before she died. If so, I would suggest writing a detailed letter and reading it aloud at the place of interment.

4. I want each family member to believe there will be help for them during the months and years ahead of them. Any suggestions or recommendations I make are put in writing, such as the list of "Crazy Feelings of Grief" (see chapter 3) and so on. I give each person a copy of my book *Experiencing Grief* and suggest they read it when they're ready. I also let them know that it is normal not to remember what they have read at this time. I send home a DVD called *Tear Soup* and ask them to watch it together.

5. There are two other family members who were lost as well—the daughter's unborn baby, and her mother-in-law. It would be easy to ignore them and gloss over this loss. I would ask the family about the baby and the mother-in-law, as well as the effect of this loss. A missing person at this time is the husband of the daughter who was killed—who is ministering to him? For the parents, their loss is a grandchild, which is major. The possible other grievers for both baby and mother-in-law would include aunts, uncles, cousins, first responders, the truck driver, friends, co-workers, pastors, church members, the ob-gyn, the husband's family and a similar group of individuals from his side of the family. It's important to consider who will minister to all of them, and how. One of our tasks as counselors is to identify neglected grievers and reach out to them as well.

6. Not only was this a sudden death, but it was also a *multiple* tragedy involving someone's child and unborn grandchild as well as the mother-in-law/grandmother of the unborn child. There could be

the possibility of legal ramifications because it was a vehicular accident. The way in which the death notification was made could be a factor as well. (For additional information on sudden death, refer to chapter 7.)

CASE 2

This is about a seven-year-old girl who called 911 to get help for her collapsed mother, performed CPR on her, but her mother died. She is now alone—she and her mother were the only ones in the home.

1. Be sure to get down on the child's level or sit next to her on the couch. Ask her name and then say, "My name is _____," and "I came over to spend some time with you to see if I could help in any way. Tell me a little about you." Just being there, being present and providing safety for the child is our task. I might ask if she has a favorite stuffed toy she would like to hold, and if so, send someone to bring it to her.

2. The child has been traumatized. Not only has she seen her mother die in front of her, but she wasn't able to save her. Here are some possible results of this experience. Her thinking process has been distorted. She could experience confusion, a distortion of time, difficulties in solving problems and in figuring out what's best to do next. In other words, as a result of trauma, something happens in her brain that affects the way she processes information. It affects how she (or any person, for that matter) interprets and stores the event she's experienced. In effect, it overrides her alarm system.

   Hypersensitivity can actually become wired into her basic brain chemistry and bodily functions. Her body is out of sync. Her heart could be pounding. She could experience nausea, cramps, sweating, headaches and even muffled hearing. Emotionally, she's riding a roller coaster. She could become irritable, afraid, anxious, frustrated, angry or simply numb.

You may eventually expect extremes of behavior—either over-responding or under-responding. Either way, her behavior may be off. She's probably slower in what she does; she wanders aimlessly and is dejected; has difficulty remembering and could be hysterical, out of control and hyper. These are all possibilities.[1] You may want to read the chapter "Guidelines to Help Children" in my book *The Complete Guide to Crisis and Trauma Counseling.*[2]

3. There are a number of practical matters, such as care-giving, for this child as well as continued counseling in the weeks ahead. It's as though you have a dual role of interacting and helping the child as well as making sure she's safe and taken care of in the future.

4. A counselor's goal is to provide support, comfort and safety for the child. There are many questions you could use to help her at this time. When you ask these it will be at your discretion.

   When children experience a crisis or trauma, it's important to help them feel free to speak their minds and to voluntarily tell you about what happened. Never force or pressure them to tell you anything they are not yet willing to verbalize. Once they feel safe and comfortable, they may want to share with you what they went through. Here is a list of what you can say to support children who are ready to tell their story. You need to talk in this manner:

   - "It's often helpful to talk about what happened."
   - "Talking about what happened can help you let go of painful thoughts and memories."
   - "Draw a picture of what's in your mind. Who would you like to spend time with now? Write a story about what's in your mind."
   - "Thoughts cannot make bad things happen or prevent them from happening."
   - "I can handle whatever you would like to tell me. Your thoughts don't scare or worry me."

- "Anything you think about is normal for what you have been through. Who would you like to tell your story to?"
- "Thinking frightening thoughts does not mean you are going crazy. What happened was crazy, but you are not."
- "What do you think happened?"
- "What do you wonder about it?"
- "What most concerned you?"
- "What's your most painful moment or memory?"
- "What was your first reaction?"
- "What's not being talked about?"
- "Are other people right or wrong about what they're saying happened?"
- "What was handled well?"
- "Who was helpful, and why?"
- "All of your thoughts before, during and after the event are normal."[3]

5. It's difficult to predict the child's questions, but here are some possibilities:

- "Did I cause my mommy's death?"
- "Isn't she just sleeping, and will she wake up soon?"
- "What happens when someone dies?"
- "Why didn't God save her?"
- "I keep hearing her breathe; when will that stop?"
- "What will happen to me now?"
- "Can I go where they're taking my mommy?"
- "What did I do wrong?"
- "Can I talk to my mommy if she's in heaven?"

I would recommend two resources you might want to take with you when you talk with children. The first is *Fears, Doubts, Blues & Pouts* by Gary Oliver and Norman Wright. This book is very readable and well illustrated on fears, worry, sadness and anger for children ages three to nine. You may have an opportunity to read one of the stories to the child, or the child could read to you. Another resource to use over an extended period of time is *A Kid's Journey of Grief* by Jo Anne Chung and Susan K. Beeney.[4]

Keep in mind that the 911 operator could be traumatized as well by this experience and may need assistance.

CASE 3

This is about a personal friend who relates that his wife's father-in-law from her first marriage has committed suicide. Her two children from that marriage have experienced four other major death losses (including their father), and now a fifth loss—their grandfather.

1. My first concern was for my friend and how this was impacting him. I said, "I hear your concern for the children, but let's talk about how this is impacting you. When you first heard the news, how did it affect you?" For a left-brain individual, I could have asked, "What did you think?" or "What went through your mind when you heard this?" For a more right-brain, feelings-oriented individual, I'd ask, "When you heard the news, what was your feeling reaction to this tragedy?" or "What went off inside of you?" In working with the teenage grandchildren, I could use some of the same responses I listed in Case 1.

2. In most cases, it is best to address the most recent loss first.

3. I could say to adult children and teenage children or grandchildren, "You've had a number of significant people die in your life. It's like an overload of dying. How are you handling this?" Initially, I would focus on the suicide. We could assume that the other family members are coming together to see you, but if one dominates the conversation, you could extend an offer to see each person individually if they so desire. Or you might break up a session and suggest that you see each one individually for a while and then together.

4. They may be at a point where they have questions, or they could still be numb and in shock. They need to know that whatever they're experiencing at this time is a normal reaction to the overload of deaths they've experienced. Often I respond with, "Given what you've been through in the past few years, losing family members, I'm just wondering what questions might be running through your mind at times?" Using such a statement/question indicates that this is what I think:

- It's all right to have questions. It's normal.
- It's safe to voice the questions.
- There's no pressure to tell me anything before they are ready (the way I asked the question and my tone takes the pressure off).
- They've been through a difficult time, and I know it.

Here are some of the questions I would expect them to think about regarding the suicide of their father/grandfather. If they do not raise these questions, I might ask, "Could it be that you may be asking . . ."

- "Why would he take his life?"
- "Why would he prefer death rather than staying here for us?"
- "Did we cause this in some way? Are we responsible?"
- "Why didn't we see this coming?"
- "Why didn't we take him more seriously? We could have prevented this."
- "Why did God let this happen?"
- "If he did this, do we have the same tendency?"

Their actual questions will also be determined by the relationship they had with their father/grandfather.

5. There are several factors to find out that may help you know how to counsel those who are grieving a suicide:

- Ask each of the members of the family to describe their relationship with their father/grandfather.

- What support system do they have in place to help them with their grief?

- What helped them get through the previous deaths? It may be helpful to have each person complete a loss history to discover which of the losses are still impacting their life (see chapter 4 in *The Complete Guide to Crisis and Trauma Counseling* for more details).

- Ask what would help them the most at this time. You can provide them with handouts such as Joanne Jozefowski's "The Crazy Feelings of Grief" (listed in chapter 3) and my book *Experiencing Grief*. You could also recommend the book *Finding Your Way After the Suicide of Someone You Love* by David Biebel and Suzanne Foster. Suggest that they consider attending a GriefShare group and contact Survivors of Suicide (SOS).

- Help them develop some responses and statements to use when others ask them questions or make comments about the suicide. I ask, "What have others said to you about your father's/grandfather's death, or what are you concerned they might say or ask?"

CASE 4

This is about a father of two adult children who is grieving the murder of one by the hand of the other.

1. This was a very difficult case. The loss of a child to murder is overwhelming enough; but the way in which it occurred and by whom it occurred is beyond comprehension. There is no way that most of us could ever grasp the torment afflicting this father. The death of a sibling by a sibling is an indescribable loss to their father—a loss that continues to grow with no end in sight. Perhaps the words that name common emotions on the "Ball of Grief" (see ball illustration

29

in chapter 6) would be only a beginning to try to describe his grief. You could make a comment like this: "I would imagine it's almost impossible to try to put into words what you've been experiencing at this time." Let's consider what this father is probably experiencing:

> When death occurs from sudden, unexpected circumstances such as accident, suicide or murder, bereavement reactions are more severe, exaggerated and complicated. The mourner's capacity to use adaptive coping mechanisms is overwhelmed.
>
> There are varied reasons for the delayed, exaggerated and complicated bereavement reactions experienced by survivors of homicide. Major characteristics experienced by survivors are cognitive dissonance—there may be disbelief and murderous impulses; conflict of values and belief system; and withdrawal of support due to the stigma of murder. Survivors must deal with feelings of fear and vulnerability, anger, rage, shame, blame, guilt and emotional withdrawal. The lack of familiarity and support by law enforcement, the criminal justice system and media intrusion also complicates bereavement. The delays in resolution of the murder conviction, lack of adequate punishment for the crime and lack of acknowledgment by society increases the feelings of loss of control.[5]

To add to this is the fact that a brother killed his sister.

2. Saying the words, "Tell me about your daughter," is a simple way to help him begin to tell his story. There is a high probability that he will jump around and talk about or ask questions concerning every aspect of what happened. Here is a simple way to help him focus: "I know how difficult it is to talk about one part of this, but it may help to structure this a bit more. Let's talk about _____ for a few minutes."

   Because of the complexity of this case, it was difficult to focus on what to grieve. He needed information and insight not just about grief but about trauma as well. Because of the notoriety of this case and the legal aspects, he can expect that his grief will continue for years. The high visibility of such a case will keep the pain at a higher level as well.

It would be good to continue to ask questions just to help him voice his pain and confusion. When there are questions for which you have no answers, simply say, "I wish we could find an answer to those questions, but right now it seems that no one has an answer."

3. This father will need others to assist him for years after this event. At this time, he may need counseling two to three times each week. Not only would a grief support group be beneficial, but also a group of those whose family member is incarcerated is needed. Encouraging him to journal daily is important to help him drain his thoughts and feelings. If he is involved in a church, develop a support group of men for him to call, spend time with, or just be available for any task or court appearance. It could take years for the case to come to trial, and there will probably be numerous delays, which will be re-traumatizing to this father (see chapters 8 and 9 of *The Complete Guide to Crisis and Trauma Counseling* for details on helping those in crises.)

4. The losses here are multiple. He has lost both children in different ways, and at some time the following will need to be addressed:

   - The fact that he may have lost someone who would have taken care of him in the future.
   - Handling the remarriage of a son-in-law or daughter-in-law—if they move, the grandchildren may be lost.
   - The significant "date" losses and developmental losses— graduation, marriage, grandchildren. He will see the other children moving on with their lives.
   - Ambiguous and disenfranchised losses—these abound in this case.
   - Loss of his own own identity.
   - No closure.

5. Since we have multiple losses, focus on one at a time. Expect to cover the same material again and again because of the complicated nature of this case. In addition, each day of the trial will be painful, so usuing a debriefing model or responding may help (see chapter 11 of *The Complete Guide to Crisis and Trauma Counseling*). Any of the other suggestions in this resource may be helpful.

Case 5

This is about a 30-year-old woman whose first husband died by accident, and whose second husband recently committed suicide. She is left with four children under the age of seven.

1. This is a case where I would expect a traumatic grief reaction. You have multiple and sudden tragic deaths, which is too much to handle, as well as having to confront the fact of caring for these children when you're least capable of doing so.

2. Here is a list of some secondary losses of relationship and support this woman may be experiencing. If the losses represented by this list sound overwhelming, they are for most people.

Secondary Losses	
friend	provider
handyman	cook
lover	bill payer
gardener	laundry person
companion	confidant
sports partner	mentor
balancer	prayer partner
mechanic	source of inspiration or insight

Secondary Losses (continued)	
identity	teacher
encourager	counselor
motivator	protector
business partner	organizer
errand person	tax preparer
couple's friends	couple's class
in-law support	feeling of safety
financial adjustment	social adjustment

3. This mother could use a team of people to assist her in some of the following areas, on a continuing basis:

   - Finances—bills, insurance, medical costs, funeral costs, sources of income
   - Assessing family resources for support
   - Prioritizing what needs to be done now and what can wait
   - Childcare support
   - Legal issues
   - Counseling support

4. The death of a spouse is difficult enough; but multiple violent and tragic deaths devastate. Here are some of the possible characteristics of her trauma:

   - *Her body could be adversely affected by some of these reactions*: chills, thirst, fatigue, nausea, fainting, twitches, vomiting, dizziness, weakness, chest pain, headaches, elevated BP, rapid heart rate, muscle tremors, shock symptoms, grinding of teeth, visual difficulties, profuse sweating, difficulty breathing.

- *Her cognitive ability may be impacted, showing some of these re-actions:* confusion, nightmares, uncertainty, hyper-vigilance, distrust; intrusive mental images; blaming others; poor problem-solving ability, poor abstract thinking, poor at-tention/decisions, poor concentration/memory; disorien-tation of time, place or person; difficulty identifying objects or people; heightened or lowered stress alertness; increased or decreased awareness of surroundings.

- *Her emotional responses are probably immobilized or charac-terized by* fear, guilt, grief, panic, denial, anxiety, agitation, irritability, depression, intense anger, apprehension, emo-tional shock, emotional outbursts, feeling overwhelmed, loss of emotional control, inappropriate emotional response.

- *The trauma might be seen in her behavior:* withdrawal; antiso-cial acts; inability to rest, intensified pacing, erratic move-ments; change in social activity; change in speech patterns; loss or increase of appetite; hyper-alert to environment; in-creased alcohol consumption; change in usual patterns of communication.

The presence of any of these symptoms may indicate the need for medical evaluation.

5. Resources for this woman should include an ongoing support sys-tem such as GriefShare, MOPS, Survivors of Suicide (SOS) and per-sonal counseling. Other resources include the books *Experiencing Grief, Finding Your Way After the Suicide of Someone You Love, Reflections of a Grieving Spouse, It's Okay to Cry* and the DVD *Tear Soup.*

Once again, it's important to remember those who may be the for-gotten grievers, such as extended family and in-laws. A major concern in this case would be the four children. Did any of those children see the body? What are their ages? The older the child, the more aware he or she might be of the circumstances of this death and the more traumatized he or she could be.

CASE 6

This is about a woman in her fifties, with multiple child loss over a period of many years: one shortly after birth, one to suicide, and one in a criminal activity.

1. Questions that I might ask or responses that I would make to help her tell her story:

   - You have experienced so many significant losses. How have you handled these?
   - I'm interested in hearing what you've been experiencing after the death of your son.
   - If someone could help you now, what would you like them to do or say to you?

This is a time to let her pour out her story of multiple losses and evaluate her coping ability, her support system, her emotional state, where she is in her grief, her questions, her faith, and so on.

Let her give the details of what others have said about a "generational curse." What is her understanding of what this means? Are these other individuals "experts" in this area, or in the area of grief? Probably not. Does this woman believe that she is under a curse? Help her clarify what she believes as well as how to respond to such statements. What is her church and theological background?

One of the main concerns is her loss of personal identity. She has "lost who she is because of what her son did." Help her amplify and clarify what she means by this. Ask her to identify all of the losses she has incurred because of this tragedy. Providing a safe place to share her story and to normalize her feelings is one of the main goals at this time.

2. Once again, this is a complicated grief situation.

   - There is the death of not just one adult son, but two.
   - They both died violently.
   - The situation involves the legal authorities.
   - She has negative support from family and others.
   - Possibly, she is feeling isolated, with no support.

3. Beginning with the death of her 12-day-old baby, years ago, ask what she did to work through the loss. What type of support did she have? What resources did she use to handle her losses? What helped her the most at that time, and what would help her now?

4. Organizations such as Compassionate Friends, Survivors of Suicide (SOS) and GriefShare would be beneficial. Identify other family members who would be supportive, as well as friends. This mother will probably need assistance in handling the comments of those who talk about a generational curse. She may need assistance in learning how to do the following: (1) how to deal with comments; (2) how to distance herself from them; and (3) how to write a letter to them stating her beliefs and requesting they do not bring up this subject again.

CASE 7

This is about a woman whose husband has just died, but his parents, with whom she had only a distant relationship, have had a hard time accepting his death and have become overly intrusive in her life.

1. Using suggestions given in the previous cases, I would respond to her grief first. I would learn as much as possible about her husband as well as their relationship. In a situation like this, sometimes I ask, "Tell me about _____ since I never had the privilege of meeting him" or "What do I need to know about _____ in order to understand the depth of your grief?" I

might ask, "If _____ were here, what would he tell me about your life together?" or "If _____ were here, what would he suggest you do to move forward in your grief?"

2. The in-laws' reaction needs to be addressed at some time, but it shouldn't override her grieving process. When you discuss it, identify who the individuals are, what the contact and interaction with them was like during the marriage, where they live, how often she will have contact with them now, as well as what kind of relationship she wants to have with them. What help are they receiving at this time with their grief, and who is available to help them? It's important to identify what type of involvement she wants with the extended family.

3. Discuss how their intrusiveness will impact her grieving. Give her guidelines and assistance on what to say to them. See the three suggestions under item 4 from Case 6.

4. Who does she have in her life to assist her in her interactions with his family?

5. What type of relationship does she want and how can she maintain that with the in-laws? If she has children, the situation is complicated because of grandparents' desires and rights, which will need to be addressed.

6. Everything that is discussed and decided upon in the counseling session needs to be in writing, with both this wife and you, the counselor, having a copy. It may be helpful to set up times when she will call you to keep you abreast of what she has done and how her interactions with the extended family have turned out.

CASE 8

This is about a woman who was away from home with her children when she was called by police and told that there was a fire in the garage and her 37-year-old husband has died of a heart attack. Her religious beliefs deny her the ability to comfort her children; and she is physically incapable of becoming the breadwinner of her home.

1. It would be helpful for you to read chapter 8, "The Phases of a Crisis," in my book *The Complete Guide to Crisis and Trauma Counseling*, which describes what this distraught wife is probably experiencing and will experience in the weeks and months to come.

2. She needs support in every way possible. Based upon the ages of the children and the fact that they saw the father dead in the garage, they may need to work with a counselor. She asks, "How am I going to survive now?" This question is a cry of despair and hopelessness. Help her identify her fears and anxieties at this time. Assist her in giving you as much information as possible about both diseases for which she has been diagnosed, such as when she was diagnosed and by whom, her symptoms, the treatments, and so on. You may need to research these conditions in order to learn as much as possible to assist. Contact your church or the national support group for each disease to assist her in this area. Reflecting her concerns and fears in your responses will be helpful. The question, "What do you think you could do at this time to help you survive?" may need to be asked more than once.

3. Differences in theology and biblical interpretations are common. When one is in a crisis state it's difficult to think and reason clearly, so it's best to assist the woman in getting her concerns out. I would turn the question about heaven back to her: "What do you believe? Is this what your husband believed?" Often, helping the person in grief clarify his/her own beliefs may take care of any questions at this time.[6]

3

The World of Grief

When we move into the world of a person in mourning, we enter a world of unpredictability, chaos and pain. We may understand what is happening from firsthand experience or just cognitively; but to effectively assist the one who mourns, we need to have a full understanding of what it's truly like to be in constant grief. Each person will have his or her own unique experience, but there are many common threads for all who mourn. Let's consider the experience. This chapter is basic, but it is fundamental to your understanding. Reflect awhile on what you read.

In grief, the bottom falls out of a person's world; the solid footing he or she once had is gone. With each step the person takes, it feels more like a floorboard tilting or soft, pliable mud. The stability of yesterday's emotions give way to feelings that are so raw and fragile that those in grief think they are losing their mind.

Mourning is another part of the experience. This is the process where grief is expressed. It's a natural, God-given process of recovery. It's His gift to us to help get us through the pain. Everyone has grief, but mourning is a choice. One cannot make his grief better, cannot make it go away, fix it or just "get over it."

There are many word pictures that others have created to describe the experience of grief. Often, when grievers read these words, they say, "Yes. That's exactly the way I feel. I thought I was the only one." They're not alone. This is normal grief.

One grieving father said:

Grief is like a wave. It comes rolling in from a far-off place. I could no more push it back than if I were standing in the water at the beach. I could not fight the wave. It moved over me and under me and broke against me, but I could never stop it. It arrived at its destination. It worked around me. The harder I fought it, the more exhausted I became. So it is with grief. If I tried to fight it, it would vanquish me. If I pushed it down it would stick in my soul and emerge as something else: depression, bitterness, exhaustion. If I yielded to the waves and let it carry me, however, it would take me to a new place.[1]

And so it is with grief. It takes a person to the top of the waves, and then the waves break, and the person struggles in the froth of emotion. It also brings memories. Grief will expose who a person really is inside. Waves run out of energy. As they move closer to the shore, their power is spent, and they slowly bubble up to the edge of the sand. The more a person stands and fights and rails against the waves, the more exhausted he or she becomes. It's an exercise in futility. But the more a person accepts it, holds out his arms to it and even embraces it, the more he will recover. People need to take a step that for many is difficult—they need to yield. They need to yield to their grief. They need to let it do its work in their life, and mourn.

When people enter into grief, they enter into the valley of shadows. There is nothing heroic or noble about grief. It's painful. It's work. It's a lingering process. But it is necessary for all kinds of losses. It has been labeled everything from intense mental anguish to acute sorrow to deep remorse.

A multitude of emotions is involved in the grief process—emotions that seem out of control and often appear in conflict with one another. With each loss come bitterness, emptiness, apathy, love, anger, guilt, sadness, fear, self-pity and a feeling of helplessness.

A Necessary Progression

Pain is a companion to grief. The pain of grief can be overwhelming. It's like a visitor who has long overstayed his welcome. No one is immune to pain, but everyone resists its intrusion.

Getting Through Denial

There are several ways that grievers attempt to resist the pain. Some fight the pain through denial. They say, "No, it isn't true," or attempt to live their lives as though nothing has happened. When they hear about the death, their first response is often, "No, that's not true. Tell me it isn't so!" or "You're mistaken." They're trying to absorb the news, and it takes time to filter through the shock. This is normal.

The author of *A Grief Disguised* said of those who are unwilling to face their pain, "Ultimately it diminishes the capacity of their souls to grow bigger in response to pain."[2]

Denial serves as emotional anesthesia and as a defense mechanism so that the survivor isn't totally overwhelmed by the loss. Denial allows them to gradually comprehend the loss, which makes it more bearable.

Grieving moves through several levels of denial. Each stage that brings home the reality of the loss is a bit deeper and more painful. A first stage is accepting it in our heads, then in our feelings; finally, we adjust life's pattern to reflect the reality of what has occurred. There is a price to pay for prolonged denial. The energy required to keep denial operating drains us, and in time, we can be damaged emotionally, delaying our recovery.

Denial is used to block out the unthinkable, but it brings with it the fear of the unknown, since it's denying the reality of what happened. As denial lessens, the pain begins to settle in; and as it does, the fear of the unknown diminishes. Denial is a cushion.

Dealing with Upheaval

Grieving is also a disorderly process. It can't be controlled, nor can it be scheduled. Grief will take the shape of a spiral figure rather than a linear one. Grief is not a straight line moving forward only to return the person to where he/she used to be. One may think they've left behind that intense pain, and the relief is so refreshing, but the pain is rediscovered again and again.

Grief disrupts your mind and your thinking ability. Confusion moves in and memory takes a vacation. If you suffer short-term memory loss after a death, it's probably a result of the stress and anxiety you are experiencing. Your life has been paralyzed and shut down. The more you accept what is occurring, the sooner it will pass.

A person may experience his last interaction with the person who died. Some say the experience is so real that it's as though they are actually there talking with the deceased person again. These experiences will pass. They're normal responses for what has occurred.

Grievers may find themselves easily distracted and perhaps disoriented even if they are usually decisive. Now they may be afraid to make choices.

Many find that their sense of time is distorted. Time goes too fast or too slow. Past and future collapse together. A clock can be sitting in front of their face but it doesn't register.

Finding a New "Normal"

To assist others with their journey of grief, we need to truly understand the world of grief. It's one of the most uncomfortable places to ever live. It hurts, confuses, upsets and frightens those who are living with it. Perhaps you've been there, but perhaps not. To effectively help someone going through grief, we must enter into this difficult world.

Whenever there is loss, there will be grief. But some do not grieve or mourn. Some make a choice not to express all the feelings inside, so their grief is accumulated. Saving it up won't lessen its pain; it will only intensify it. Silence covers a wound before the cleansing has occurred. The result will be an emotional infection.

Some try to make others carry their burden. But grief can't be shared. Everyone has to carry it alone and in his or her own way.[3]

Grief is slow, and it needs to be this way, even though most people probably want to rush it along. It will take longer than anyone has patience for. Time seems to stand still, especially at night; but the slowness of grief is necessary.

Everyone grieves and heals differently. Some want to be connected to people as much as possible. Others prefer to be left alone. Some prefer to take care of their own problems, while others want assistance. One prefers activity, while another prefers just the opposite. Others may attempt to fill their lives with what they don't want.

Even though it will take effort, those who grieve may need to let others know what they need and the best way for others to help them. When grief is a close companion, it's experienced in many ways. It permeates and changes feelings, thoughts and attitudes.

Good Reasons to Mourn

Why does everyone have to go through this experience? What is the purpose?

- Through grief we express our feelings about our loss.
- Through grief we express our protest at the loss as well as our desire to change what happened and have it not be true. This is a normal response.
- Through grief we express the effects we have experienced from the devastating impact of the loss.[4]
- Through grief we may experience God in a new way that changes our life. As Job said, "My ears had heard of you before, but now my eyes have seen you" (Job 42:5, NCV).

The following is an excerpt from one of my counseling sessions that illustrates the importance of going through the mourning process:

Ted: Why do I have to go through all this pain . . . No, not pain, agony of grief—it's plain, pure agony, and I hate it. Everyone tells me I need to mourn—I have to complete my "mourning" in order to move on, whatever that means. Go ahead;

convince me. You're the expert. You're the teacher. Give me some good reasons . . . and don't turn it back on me and ask me to come up with them myself like you usually do. [We both laughed.] This is one time when you have to talk and give me some direct guidance . . . And just think, what you say you could share with others or in your teaching or, imagine this, Norm . . . one of your books! [More laughter]

Norm: First, it's probably one of the best things you can do for yourself as well as for others in your life. Right now you feel out of control. [He nods.] It's a way to regain some control of your life. In order to develop a new, healthy relationship with Jean, it needs to change. You've said that your emotions are raging out of control. This is one way to regain control.

I know you want to be healthy. Completing your mourning, which you've said before you don't think is possible, will give you back your health, which has been impacting your loss. And I've talked not just about the physical area but about the psychological as well as the spiritual.

In order to move on in life, and we've talked about this before, you need to learn to live without the one you've lost. We know that's an ongoing process. With the loss of a loved one, one's identity is not only changed but damaged. When you mourn, you will begin to form new beliefs and rebuild a new sense of meaning for your life. Right now, when you think about Jean, you hurt. Mourning is what will bring you to the place where someday you'll think about Jean without any hurt. Finally, it's the only way I know to overcome what you've been experiencing and relearn your new life.

During seasons of grief, the days seem like night, often with a blanket of fog swishing about. The psalmist reflected this when he said, "When my spirit was overwhelmed within me" (Ps. 142:3, *KJV*). These words literally mean, "The muffling of my spirit." But as grief begins to thaw, they will find the sun breaking through their gloom. The psalmist said, "Weeping may remain for a night, but rejoicing comes in the morning" (Ps. 30:5).

Perhaps one of the best descriptions of grief comes from Joanne T. Jozefowski's book *The Phoenix Phenomenon: Rising from the Ashes of Grief.* These characteristics or symptoms, with such a fitting title, seem to resonate with almost everyone I've shared them with; and all too often, I hear, "Yes. Every one of these symptoms describes what my life is like right now."

The Crazy Feelings of Grief

The "crazy" feelings of grief are actually a sane response to grief. The examples on the following page are all symptoms of normal grief. I would encourage you to print this listing and share it with those you are working with.

The passage of grief will take longer than one could ever imagine. It tends to intensify at three months, on special dates and on the one-year anniversary.[5]

Grief takes on many faces, such as disruption, holes, confusion. It disrupts one's entire life schedule. And the ensuing grief doesn't just impact one part of a person. It comes from within and doesn't leave one particle of life untouched. It's all-consuming. There are body changes. Food doesn't taste the same, nor will the fragrance of a favorite flower be as intense. The frequency of tears clouds vision. Some experience a tightness in their throat or chest, an empty feeling in their stomach, shortness of breath or rapid heart rate. Eating and sleeping patterns won't be the same. Some people sleep and sleep, while others wish that sleep would come. Sleep is either an easy escape or it's elusive. Dreams or nightmares occur. This disruption will decrease in time, but recovery is not a smooth, straightforward path; it's a forward-backward dance.

If grief occurs because of the death of a loved one, the person's life has now been divided into two segments—life before the death and life

The Crazy Feelings
of Grief

- Distorted thinking patterns, "crazy" and/or irrational thoughts, fearful thoughts

- Feelings of despair and hopelessness

- Out of control or numbed emotions

- Changes in sensory perceptions (sight, taste, smell, and so forth)

- Increased irritability

- May want to talk a lot or not at all

- Memory lags and mental "short-circuits"

- Inability to concentrate

- Obsessive focus on the loved one

- Losing track of time

- Increase or decrease of appetite and/or sexual desire

- Difficulty falling or staying asleep

- Dreams in which the deceased seems to visit the griever

- Nightmares in which death themes are repeated

- Physical illness like the flu, headaches or other maladies

- Shattered beliefs about life, the world, and even God

after. Grief can also bring out the best in a person as well as the worst.

Many people you help will ask you, "What is wrong with me?" Their thoughts trail off; their concentration is nonexistent and memory deficits are the norm.

Prior to the death of a loved one, life was going in a well-established direction. This has changed. Before the death, there was an identity. They could say who they were. This, too, has changed. They are not exactly who they were. The person who died was part of their identity. They were someone's mother or aunt or spouse or brother. They continue to be that person in their heart and memory, but there's a vacant place where the loved one stood. The loss of this person has subtracted from them part of who they were. Eventually, they will take steps to move from the old to the new identity.[6] This may be hard to grasp now, but someday . . .

Some may also experience the "face in the crowd" syndrome. They think they have seen the one they lost or heard their voice or smelled their perfume or cologne. This can happen at home or in public places. They may wake up at night and swear they sensed their presence in the room or heard them call their name. They think they're going crazy and hesitate to share the experience with others for fear of what they will think. But this is more common than most realize and can last for as long as 18 months.

Additional Losses

It is not just the loss of the loved one that is so painful. It is also all the other losses that occur because of the one who has died: the way they lived their life, loved, slept, ate, worked and worshiped are all affected. Often the death of the loved one brings up not just grief for what has been lost but also for what they never had and what they never will have.

There is a loss of the present as well as the future. This especially impacts relationships. They may feel awkward around others for whom the one they lost was also a loved one. A death can put distance in some relationships or draw together and connect others in a greater intimacy than before. Death can be a wedge or source of confusion. Those in grief may feel disconnected with others, and as they feel alienated they may tend to withdraw, which reinforces their feelings. This can lead to a belief that "others just don't understand," which is often true.

The process of grief involves saying goodbye to the old life. This occurs with the acknowledgment that the loved one is truly gone and won't return. Many grievers struggle with holding on while trying to let go. The ongoing task is to develop a new way of relating to the one who died.

There are behavior changes. Many say, "I'm just not myself." That's true. They won't be for some time. They may find themselves zoning out when others are talking. Their mind drifts off since it's difficult to stay focused and attentive. They feel detached from people and activities even though they're an important part of their life. What is upsetting to many is how absentminded they are. They may cry for "no apparent" reason. It's common to lose their sense of awareness of where they are, relating both to time and place.

Whether the death was expected or sudden, one may experience numbness. The more unexpected and traumatic the loss, the more intense the numbness will be. At first, feelings are muted, like muting the sound on a TV. The initial shock of knowing a loved one is dead puts most into a paralyzing state of shock. This is a period in which no mourner can describe things clearly, thanks to nature's protection measures. Shock is a natural protection, as though someone gave the person anesthesia. It insulates them from the intensity of the feelings of loss, but it also may prevent them from understanding the full experience of the loss.

There will be a time when feelings could be described as a time of suffering and disorganization, or even chaos. The trance is over. We talk about scenes rather than stages, for stages vary depending on whom you read. And there are those who bypass some scenes. After the numbness wears off, the pain of separation comes. Sometimes those who grieve wish they could go back to the initial stage of numbness or shock. At least there the pain wasn't so intense. There is an intense longing for the return of the person that was lost—for the sight of them, the sound of them, their smell and just knowing he or she could walk through that door again. One person described the loss of a loved one as "like having a tree that has been growing in one's heart yanked out by its roots, leaving a gaping hole or wound."[7] And the question begins to form: "Why?"

The griever may ask or even shout "Why?" countless times a day at this point. Many wonder, *Do I have the right to ask why?* It's not just a question; it's a heart-wrenching cry of protest. It's the reaction of "No, this shouldn't be! It isn't right!"

Job, in the Bible, asked that question 16 times. And there are others. Listen to their cries:

Why, O LORD, do you stand far off? Why do you hide yourself in times of trouble? (Ps. 10:1).

How long, O LORD? Will you forget me forever? How long will you hide your face from me? How long must I wrestle with my thoughts and every day have sorrow in my heart? How long will my enemy triumph over me? (Ps. 13:1-2).

My God, my God, why have you forsaken me? (Matt. 27:46).

Ken Gire writes: "Painful questions, all of them. Unanswered questions, many of them. And we, if we live long enough and honestly enough, one day we will ask them, too."[8]

It's not unusual to struggle to pray. At times it's as though the words stick in the mind and can't get past the lips. The questions, concerns, pleas and requests are there, but they derail when one attempts to express them to God.

It's important for us as counselors to validate this spiritual struggle. "Why?" is not only a question but a cry of protest, and there really is no answer at this time. (See *A Sacred Sorrow*, by Michael Card, for a complete presentation on the value of lamenting and asking "why?").

Clusters of Feelings that Come and Go

One of the clusters of feelings to emerge will be a sense of emptiness, loneliness and isolation, even when others are next to the person in grief. Invisible boundaries have been erected. In two or three months' time, there will be even more loneliness and isolation as friends and family pull away.

The second common cluster of feelings is fear and anxiety. And the fears accumulate. They may come and go or be a constant sense of dread. It's a common response whenever we face the unknown and the unfamiliar. These feelings range from the fear of being alone, to fear of the future, of additional loss, of desertion or abandonment.

Fear works as an alarm system that warns survivors of major changes in their understanding and assumptions regarding themselves and others.[9] Anxiety awakens an awareness of a person's inability to control events. The person may feel that he or she should have been able to prevent or at least predict the occurrence of the loss. "What will I do?" is a phrase that expresses fear. The greater the emotional investment in the one who was lost, the more the griever will tend to feel like a ship adrift at sea.

One fear is that if they stop wanting the person to return, they will stop loving him or her. In addition, the worst agony of intense grief occurs when a person realizes that the return they want more than anything else is the one thing they can't have.[10]

Some have said, "You need to let go of the loved one completely." But consider the thinking of the author of *The Heart of Grief*:

> Grieving persons who want their loved ones back need to look for some other way to love them while they are apart. Desperate longing prevents their finding that different way of loving. Letting go of having them with us in the flesh is painful and necessary. But it is not the same as completely letting go. We still hold the gifts they gave us, the values and meanings we found in their lives. We can love them as we cherish their memories we found in their lives. We can love them as we treasure

their legacies in our practical lives, and spirits. But there is nothing in all of this that implies that we must let go completely. There is no reason to let go of the good with the bad.[11]

Those who grieve may wake up and ask, "How can I face the day without him (her)?" They are afraid of being on their own. There may be anxiety over dealing with the pain of the separation. They may be upset over the realization that they're a different person. They're "without" someone. Many worry over how other family members will cope and survive. Since they've lost one person, what if they lose another family member or friend, especially if the current loss was sudden and unexpected?

Guilt and shame walk their way into the grief process. There are numerous sources for the guilt. The most immediate guilt comes from taking some responsibility for the loss, or perhaps it is connected to a discussion they feel contributed to the loss in some way. Guilt is possibly the most difficult emotion to handle. It's often tied into unrealistic expectations. Many grievers hold themselves responsible for events over which they have no control, such as thinking they could have done something different or done something more in order to prevent the death. Guilt could also be leftover unfinished business they wish they had attended to, and it leads to regret that turns into guilt.

Some continue to live in the land of regrets and let their lives become a continuous self-recriminating statement. And the regrets seem to grow. They tie into *shoulds* as well. "I should have said . . . done . . . known . . ." Guilt may occur because of unresolved negative feelings over things they did or didn't do. It's common in the early phases of grief to recall all that was negative in a relationship while failing to remember the positives equally as well. There is another tendency at this time. They may dwell on all the bad or negative things they think they did in their relationship with the person they lost while also over focusing on all the good things the deceased did. And then there is "survivor guilt." The person in grief feels guilty because he or she is still alive.

Guilt is an unpredictable emotion, and that in itself creates guilt. Some experience guilt because they're not recovering according to their timetable. This is where "should" and "if only" come to mind. When a death is unexpected or sooner than anticipated, the tendency to blame rushes to the forefront. After we've blamed others, it's easy to transfer the blame to ourselves. "If only I had . . ." The list is endless.

Some imagine that if they had done something differently they could have prevented the death. If suicide was the cause of death, this feeling could be overwhelming.

A feeling of anger is a feeling of displeasure, irritation and protest. In grief it's often a protest, a desire to make someone pay, to declare the unfairness of the death when frustrated, hurt, afraid or feeling helpless. Anger/hostility acts as a protective self-defense emotion that demands the world be predictable and operate according to one's expectations. Sometimes the anger is expressed like a heat-seeking missile. It can erupt suddenly without warning.

Anger is a response to hurt or pain. It can be pain in the past, present or future. When the pain is in the past, there is resentment. It's not uncommon to experience these feelings even toward the one who died. When direct expression is blocked, it leaks out and gets invested elsewhere. If it is invested against oneself, it can turn into depression.

It may be especially hard for some people to admit being angry at God, perhaps for not responding in the way the person wanted; or angry because their faith and beliefs didn't seem to work. This kind of distress over the failure of God to respond in a desired way can prolong the grief process.

Finally, there is the sense of sadness, depression and despair. Depression makes each day look as though the dark clouds are here to stay. Apathy blankets the person like a shroud, and withdrawal becomes a lifestyle. When depression hits, accurate perspective leaves. Depression will alter relationships because of being oversensitive to what others say and do. Jeremiah the prophet displayed these feelings: "Desperate is my wound. My grief is great. My sickness is incurable, but I must bear it" (Jer. 10:19, *TLB*). The deeper the depression, the more paralyzing the sense of helplessness. Depression can also affect us spiritually and can change the way we see God.

Some have said that grief is the blackest night of confusion because of all the emotion. The anger of feelings is like a smorgasbord. Each day there's a wide variety to choose from. There will be daily variations of emotion that come and go. Just when you think they're gone for good, they come again and overlap one another. Over time these emotions come less frequently and less intensely.

Our thoughts are not immune from grief. Most people would like more control over them, but that's difficult. Preoccupation with the death and its pain can sweep in when a person least expects it—when in a group, when attempting to work through a business transaction or when driving—which could lead to a ticket or an accident.

It's true that we can hold back and bottle up feelings, but not for long. If we don't let them out, we'll discover that they'll find their own means of expression.

One of the secret feelings of grief is relief. Few would admit to this. It's an "I shouldn't be experiencing this" type of feeling mixed in with all the other responses. I'll talk more about this in chapter 6.

At the conclusion of most of the chapters, you will find a portion of an actual verbatim transcript from a counseling session. Permission has been granted to use these, and names have been changed. There are several additional transcripts in the appendix. You may learn more about grief counseling and coaching from reading these sessions of counseling than from other portions of the book. As you read, keep asking yourself, "What was the purpose of the counselor's response?" and "What could I have said differently?" There are many ways to respond. So study and reread the case studies and responses more than once. They can also be used as a teaching tool for groups of counselors and lay counselor training.

Phil

Counselor: Would you like to give us some information on the situation, Phil?

Phil: I'll give you some background. My nephew is a quadriplegic. He lives over in Oceanside. He broke his neck 16 years ago, at the age of 18, right after he graduated. He dove into the water at Laguna Beach and hit a sandbar and broke his neck, and he can't move from his shoulders down. He's been suicidal lately, and I've offered to help and assist. Unfortunately, they told me he wouldn't talk to anybody. And neither could I get the parents to allow me to come over to talk with them. That is the difficult part. The parents wouldn't talk to me on the phone, but his mother did email me; she's my wife's sister. It's her son that broke his neck. He stopped eating, and this is the third time he has attempted to take his life. He's been insisting that his parents sign a piece of paper so that if he ends up in the hospital it will allow him to tell them that he doesn't want a feeding tube or respirator or anything. He's on a full-time respirator now, so he can't breathe without it. He's at home with his mom and dad; they do have a nurse come in every day for 12 hours, and then mom and dad take over after that when they come home from work. So I think it's more than they can handle at this point. My recommendation in an email was that they seek help either from a chaplain from the police department, fire department or wherever. I suspect that this kind of help is needed at this point in time. I don't know how to get through to him because he won't let anyone talk to him.

Counselor: If you were to talk to him, would he respond?

Phil: At this point, he's not responding to his parents. And that's their concern. But I keep telling them, "You don't know if he would respond to me. He might not be responding to you because he's angry with you because you won't grant his wish to take his life." I could find out what the extent of it is.

Counselor: What is his name?

Phil: Seth.

Counselor: Phil, if you were to go there and talk to Seth, what would you say? How would you approach it?

Phil: The first thing I would ask is, "Seth, are you feeling hurt?" I don't think he's been asked that. Because I do know some of the situation that brought this on is that one of the male nurses that he really liked and had a good relationship with just up and left. At that point in time is when he went downhill really fast.

Counselor: So he probably feels abandoned.

Phil: Yes.

Counselor: And when you talk with him you're looking for the emotional hurt.

Phil: Correct [nodding].

Counselor: Let's say that Seth doesn't say anything.

Phil: I suspect he won't respond.

Counselor: How will you respond if he doesn't say anything?

Phil: That's where I've been stumped.

Counselor: What are some possibilities?

Phil: Well, I think that some possibilities [pausing to think] might be bringing up, "Seth, are you hurt because of losing _____?" I could see if that would trigger a response out of him. He has two high-school friends who have kept in touch, and they keep calling and calling but he won't answer their calls and he won't talk to them. He's put a blog on the computer that says, "my parents won't allow me to commit suicide; somebody please help me." So he's crying out for help. So I'm not sure if he will accept the help. It seems like his parents aren't allowing him to get outside help. Outside help is what I think both his parents and he need at this time.

Counselor: Would it be possible to say to him, "I have noticed that you are crying out for help. You've asked for help in committing suicide and wanting your parents' help there. In what other ways can your parents help, or anyone help you, if suicide wasn't going to occur? If you continue to be alive, what would make living better for you?"

Phil: That's where I want to take the conversation. Find out what will make it better for him. If you stop and think, he's bedridden all the time, and he needs help with everything. He does have a power chair that he can operate with his mouth. He has been able to get into the power chair and go out with a nurse beside him. He nearly ran the power chair off a cliff. That's when the nurse reached over and powered it off and then was able to manually move it and take it away from the cliff and take him home. The nurse thought that maybe he wanted to get out and see the view, but then when he started increasing the power, the nurse knew this was more than a walk. The parents have threatened to commit him to a hospital. They use the term 51/50; I'm not familiar with it. I guess it means they can exercise the right to have someone committed who is a danger to himself. The parents have also asked, "Would you like to go see your favorite doctor?" and he hasn't responded. He hasn't had any fluids for about three weeks.

Counselor: Phil, how will you handle it when you go talk to him? Let's assume you're going to talk to him. How are you going to respond if he doesn't respond to you?

Phil: I am going to let him know, and let his parents know, that he needs serious help. I am going to recommend that help needs to come from outside the home.

Counselor: Before you get to that point, are you going to continue to try to engage him?

Phil: Yes, continually. I have continued with the conversations with his mom and dad, but I'm not getting anywhere with them. The biggest problem is that they are Jehovah's Witnesses and they know that I am a Christian. They do not want me to come over and talk about the Bible. I've made it perfectly clear that I won't do that; I will only use the training I have received here. And from a sense of urgency of really wanting to help Seth, more than anything else.

Counselor: Let's say they give you permission and they understand you're not going to proselytize. How will you handle Seth's non-response to you? You'd like him to respond, but chances are he won't. How do you deal with the feelings you're experiencing with him not saying anything?

Phil: I would probably relate to him the times I've felt that kind of despair and let him know the feelings I've had.

Counselor: Good.

Phil: I'd let him know the times I've been suicidal in the past. I would let him know what helped me. Obviously, what helped me was different, because I have the physical ability to get up and do things while he does not. So what helped me may not necessarily help him. I would start talking there and see if it might generate some response, watching his eyes to see if there is any response at all.

Counselor: So you'd be telling your story. One other suggestion would be to take the pressure off of you in your heart and mind to give Seth permission not to say anything to you, not to respond. Because what you are doing is not dependent upon him starting to talk to you.

Phil: Right.

Counselor: A positive part of this is you having the opportunity to share. You don't know what is going to penetrate. So maybe it's a matter of knowing ahead of time, "Here are some things I'd like to leave with you, things that I'd like you to consider." I see this similar to ministering to a stroke victim in the hospital when you continue to talk, pray, talk, read scripture with no response . . . and months later when they come out of it they say, "Thank you for what you did."

Phil: I had that experience, unfortunately, with my daughter who died of cancer. Just before she died, we thought she was in a coma, and I spent the day talking with her and reading Scripture to her. I got to a specific Scripture and she said the name Jesus and came out of the coma for a day or two. Then she died shortly after that. So I firmly believe they can hear when they're in a coma.

Counselor: [nodding and encouraging Phil to go on]

Phil: You just have to continue to talk and share; I kept her up to date as to what was going on with the rest of the family at that time, as well as some quiet time for herself and reading her Scripture.

Counselor: It sounds like you have been through quite a bit yourself.

Phil: Oh, a tad bit. Right after my daughter died, my wife and I had been with her in Boise, Idaho. We had been there for a month trying to take care of her and to get things ready because we knew she was dying. The tough part was trying to get pain control. She had to have a spinal, and they put it in the wrong area to start with. The fluid ended up around her liver, and she really got jaundiced and bloated real bad. They continued to increase her fluid because the pain wasn't going away, but it wasn't going to the right spot. When we finally saw the pain doctor, he saw it was in the wrong spot and put it in the correct area. At that point in time she was given too much, and although she was pain free, she was completely paralyzed from the waist down. The doctor warned us that she could stop breathing because the medication might get up into her lungs. So my wife stayed up with her all night. We took turns staying awake with her. We were exhausted by the time we were able to get her into a hospice home. About two weeks after we got home, I had a heart attack and I had to have bypass surgery. My wife found a lump on her breast and she had breast cancer. So we went through quite a trauma during that time. I had complications and had to have my chest open 3 times in 30 hours. When I came out of it the third time, my right lung was not fully inflated and my left lung was filled with water, and I had pneumonia. I nearly didn't make it. My wife went through that trauma with me. It was a long road home. And since then I've had to redo bypass surgery, about three years ago now. So I've struggled with that, but God's brought me through every time and used me in a mighty way. As a result, to minister to people, and I'm grateful for that. I'm really praying that He will use me with Seth.

Counselor: Does Seth know your whole story?

Phil: Yes.

Counselor: I would encourage you to just keep trying to have an audience with Seth. You never know what you say and how it will affect him. You indeed are a survivor.

Phil: Yes.

Counselor: How can I best pray for you at this time?

Phil: That the opportunity opens up that I can minister to Seth or that he at least would start taking some food and water. And that God would minister to this family and allow them to open up to intervention if needed. And to help them, because I know that Seth's mom and dad are exhausted from all of this and they need help as well.

Counselor: That might be another area for ministry—your ministry to his parents. I would also like to pray that there would be the opportunity for openness to the gospel, where Seth could hear something from Joni Eareckson Tada. What she has been through and how through this experience lives have been changed throughout the world because of her wheelchair ministry. She has written an excellent chapter on suffering in the book *Suffering and the Sovereignty of God* by John Piper. It's just amazing. Thank you for being so transparent with me.

Phil: Thank you for the opportunity.

Analysis

This was a complicated case. Initially, the counselor worked with Phil on structuring some type of plan to help Seth. Sometimes the counselee knows what to do but just needs the guiding comments to sort through and gain direction. Some of the remarks from the counselor are actually teaching responses, but the emphasis here was helping Phil figure out what to do. Since Phil's focus was on Seth, we didn't explore Phil's losses or previous suicidal intention. This session was more cognitive than emotional in nature. If you were to explore Phil's losses, what would you say? What are all the losses you can identify based on what Phil told the counselor?

4

Models of Grief

The journey of grief and all its stops and starts has been given many descriptive faces, from the "Five Stages of Grief" model by Elizabeth Kübler-Ross to William Worden's four "Tasks of Grief," which need to be worked through during the grief journey. Joanne Jozefowski speaks about the difference in the patterns of grief in her book *The Phoenix Phenomenon: Rising from the Ashes of Grief*:

> Although there are predictable and universal aspects of grieving, each person's experience is unique. The phases and their tasks are most often described in chronological sequence, but in reality, they assume a "hopscotch" sequence: individuals may proceed through two or three phases only to find themselves back to "start" some six months later.
>
> Some grievers may experience several phases almost simultaneously. For instance, a grieving person who is also the family provider may have to return to work immediately and must adapt to life without the loved one while experiencing symptoms of shock, anger, profound sorrow, depression, and all else that follows. For others, the phases overlap and may be re-experienced later on in the grief cycle or many years afterward. This is the *rhythm* of grief.[1]

We need to remember the uniqueness of each griever and *not* try to make them fit our model.

"Tasks of Grief"

One of the models that has been helpful to me is the five-step task approach of Dr. Susan J. Zonnebelt-Smeenge and Dr. Robert C. DeVries. They talk about tasks as five interrelated goals that need to be accomplished or experienced for a person to move through the grief process into a new life. In one sense it's another way of saying "relearning their world." This is what Zonnebelt-Smeenge and DeVries say about the tasks in one of their books:

> They are not sequential in the sense that one task needs to be completed before you begin another. In fact, they are complexly interrelated like a fine symphony, with parts of one task being worked on simultaneously with others. They are not the type of tasks that can be completed quickly or all at once—these tasks are integral to your entire grieving process.
>
> This grief process is like putting a complex puzzle together. There are as many ways of accomplishing this as there are individuals doing it. However, there *are* designated puzzle pieces to be used in specific relationship to others. Only when the puzzle is complete can a person sit back and appreciate the entire picture for what is and declare it to be finished. That is also true of the grief process—it is an individual journey, yet there are the five specific tasks with corresponding behaviors that you need to address to help you move through your grief detour.
>
> So what are these tasks that are necessary to heal from grief?

- *First*, you need to accept the reality that your loved one has died and is unable to return. This may seem obvious, but emotionally accepting the reality of the death can be a tremendous challenge.

- *Second,* you need to express all your emotions associated with the death. Keeping the emotions "bottled up" inside yourself can complicate your grief journey.

- *Third,* you need to sort through and identify the memories of your loved one and find a place to store them so you can begin to move on. This task basically means that because your loved one is no longer present—no longer a dynamic and active part of your ongoing journey—you need to make him or her a vital and rich memory of your life.

- *Fourth,* identify who you are independent of your deceased loved one. If you experienced the death of your second parent, are you now an orphan? If a child died, how do you answer the question, "How many children do you have?" When your spouse dies, are you still married? Or widowed? Or single? Reworking your sense of identity is a critical aspect of your grief journey.

- *Finally,* the grief detour requires that you begin to reinvest in your life in a way that is consistent with your reshaped sense of identity—determining your own personal interests and desires at this point in your life.[2]

Consider how you might make use of this task model as you sit with those in grief and walk with them on their journey. Sometimes you can explain it outright while other times it's just a matter of identifying the tasks on our part. What questions can you think of to bring out this information?

"Cries of Grief"

There is another model that is worth considering. It's not that the various models stand alone. There is a blending and intertwining of the various suggestions. Your task is to weave together all this information to use when you minister. The more you know, the more you can fill your reservoir of knowledge and the more you can draw upon.

Dr. Merton P. Strommen and his wife, Irene, in their book about the death of their son, share five different responses they experienced in their grief. These are different facets of grief; they are not linear stages to work through, but various degrees of intensity. They are called "The Cries of Grief."

Pain

There is a *cry of pain* that can bring one to his knees. For many it's as if something has been wrenched or torn out of them. This pain can be within the body as well as in the emotions. It will come and go, often for years, as well as for no apparent reason.

As one father said about the loss of his son:

> The intensity of pain will diminish, but the loss haunts us to the end. But since loss and grief are a part of life, strangely enough the sorrow becomes a kind of minor chord along with the jubilant majors to give life a new richness. It would be far more difficult if we could not believe that our sons are a part of that great bleacher company, the cloud of witnesses, now cheering us on from the other side.[3]

Using the concept of degrees of intensity of pain, rather than stages, here are three questions to ask the one being counseled:

1. How would you describe the pain you're experiencing at this time?
2. Where in your body are you experiencing the pain?
3. When is your pain the worst and when is there some relief?

Longing

There is also a *cry of longing*—this comes from the sense of emptiness and loneliness that exists because of the loss of a loved one. For many this is a longing they've never experienced before. It can occur at a special time of the year or when certain events occur or for no apparent reason. For some, wherever they go, even if it's enjoyable, there is that feeling of "I wish he or she were here." The longing may come out in cries of "Where are you? Why did you leave? Why now?" There's an intense desire to see and hear the loved one once again.

With this cry of intensity, you could ask:

1. When is the time that you long for your loved one the most?
2. What has helped you the most during your times of loneliness?

Supportive Love
A third cry is for *supportive love*. One of the worst experiences is to feel all alone, isolated in a world full of people. Those in grief have some specific needs for love and support. They need family members to support them, especially those who are healthy emotionally and can be encouraging. They also need others who accept what has happened, who care and who can help with what needs to be done in terms of daily tasks. They need people to reach out for months and years later with care and concern. They need others to talk about the deceased, share memories and use the deceased person's name. Continuous support and love is a priority.

For counseling purposes, you can use these types of questions:

1. When are the times when you feel isolated or all alone?
2. How would you like others to respond to you at this time?
3. Who are the people you would like involved in your life at this time, and who are those with whom you would prefer not to be involved?

Understanding
William Barclay said, "The hardest lesson of all . . . is to accept what one cannot understand and still say, 'God, thou art love. I build my faith on that.' "[4] This is a cry to accept what has happened, but often the desire to comprehend is overwhelmed. Often one's relationship with God

becomes disrupted for a while. For many, their desire is to try to make time stand still, to keep things as they were, to return to a previous time.

As one grieving father said:

> I was bothered by seemingly contradictory emotions. How could I laugh when I was feeling so sad? How could I be resentful of what happened and yet accept it? How could I let go and still hang on? How could I believe and doubt in the same breath? How could I actually experience deep joy, and yet feel the unutterable pain of having lost?[5]

The cry of *why* is the cry of lament. This is a cry that is good. It is necessary. It is a cry of protest to God, but also a cry of faith. Michael Card's book *A Sacred Sorrow* describes how lament is a biblical pattern for our lives. He states:

> When then, does God enshrine so many laments in His Word? Laments, we must realize *are* God's Word. Why are so many biblical characters shown as disappointed and angry with God? Do we seek to learn from all the other facets of their lives but this? I would put it to you this way. People like Job, David, Jeremiah, and even Jesus reveal to us that prayers of complaint can still be prayers of faith. They represent the last refusal to let go of the God who may seem to be absent or worse—uncaring. If this is true, then lament expresses one of the most intimate moments of faith—not a denial of it. It is supreme honesty before a God whom my faith tells me I can trust. He encourages me to bring everything as an act of worship, my disappointment, frustration and even my hate. Only lament uncovers this kind of new faith, a biblical faith that better understands God's heart as it is revealed through Jesus Christ.[6]

He also talks about the purpose of lamenting:

> What lament would have us understand the answer is being graciously given. His Presence is always with us. Lament is the path

that takes us to the place where we discover that there is no complete answer to pain and suffering, only Presence. The language of lament gives a meaningful form to our grief by providing a vocabulary for our suffering and then offering it to God as worship. Our questions and complaints will never find individual answers (even Job's questions were never fully answered). The only Answer is the dangerous, disturbing, comforting Presence, which is the true answer to all our questions and hopes.[7]

This book is a valuable and insightful resource for anyone involved in grief counseling. Its exploration of the language of weeping (lament) found in the Bible—pouring out the heart in anger, pain and sorrow—expands our view of worship and our understanding of what God says is appropriate language to engage Him with.

1. What questions do you have about your loss at this time?
2. Who or what has helped you with your questions?
3. How can you handle the questions that will never be answered?

Significance

A final cry is the *cry for significance*, the desire to see something good eventually come out of this loss. It's the process of transforming grief into growth.[8]

Grieving is a matter of beginning with the question, "Why did this happen to me?" and eventually moving on to "How can I learn through this experience? How can I now go on with my life?" When the *how* question replaces the *why* question, one has started to live with the reality of the loss. *Why* questions reflect a search for meaning and purpose in loss. *How* questions reflect searching for ways to adjust to the loss.[9]

The eventual goal is to be able to say, "This loss I've experienced is a crucial upset in my life. In fact, it is the worst thing that will ever happen to me. But is it the end of my life? No. I can still have a rich, fulfilling life. Grief has been my companion and has taught me much. I can use it to grow into a stronger person than I was before my loss."

Questions to ask when the counselee is seeking significance in the loss:

1. What meaning, if any, have you discovered through this death?
2. How are you different because of this loss experience?
3. Two years from now, what will you be like?
4. What have you discovered about God through this experience?

As you work with those in grief, look for these five cries of intensity. They're not isolated but are intertwined and overlap. Any or all may be useful for you and the griever to explore.

It's true that there are tasks to accomplish, cries to pour out and the learning of how to move on. Grief is also about relearning your world. The world of those left behind is changed. It is not the same, nor will it be the same as much as those in grief wish it would be. So, in addition to the loss of the person, there is the loss of the familiar. The task at hand for each one in grief is to relearn this new world. It involves learning how to respond as a different person as well as how to act. Those around us will need to relearn our new world as well, because each griever is different in more ways than he or she even realizes.

Their loss of a loved one is the total disruption of the life they knew; in a sense, they have now been forced to start over.

Those in grief have to relearn their *physical surroundings* strange as it sounds. Their personal life has taken on a different meaning as do objects, routings, our favorite places; the new absence puts a strain on everyday interactions. It's not just that a loved one was lost, but other loved ones were lost as the griever once knew them, for their grief made them different too. The various roles the person fulfilled prior to their death must be identified and substitutes found.[10]

Grievers need to learn *who they are* at this time. It's a time of forced discovery of how they cope, think about themselves, who they are spiritually, the emotions they experience or don't experience, how they feel now about others, what that means to them and what has lost its significance. This will be a time of personal disappointment as well as encouragement based on these discoveries. When loss invades one's life, a person is never the same; for when their world changes, they change in many ways, some of which challenge, threaten, disappoint and surprise. Many people, especially in early stages of grief, wonder if their life will ever be whole again. It can be a time of tremendous change and growth, especially spiritual change and growth.

Thomas Attig describes the various types of struggles that grievers experience. Each of these struggles provides us with a direction or question to use as we engage the person during counseling.

Grievers struggle to relieve the distress and anguish of suffering. It's common to become paralyzed by the suffering. Thus we ask:

- "How would you describe the suffering you've been experiencing?"
- "What value, if any, do you see in this suffering, either now or in the future?"
- "What causes you the greatest distress at this time? What has helped you the most, if anything, in handling this?"

Grievers struggle to restore whatever they can that still remains from their previous life pattern. We ask:

- "In what ways is your life both different as well as the same before _____ died?"
- "What has worked for you in bringing back some of your previous life at this time?"

Grievers struggle to change themselves and discover a new way of living which gives meaning to their life. We ask:

- "In the midst of all this chaos, what have you discovered that is giving you a new sense of meaning?"

- "What have you learned at this point in time which will give you meaning in this new life without _____?"[11]

Because a griever's life story has been disrupted, this person experiences incompleteness in his or her self. The person's story is unraveled, for the expectations and hopes about how the story ends or will continue have come to a halt. The past that gave meaning and purpose may become too painful to remember; the present overly confusing; and the future cloudy and uncertain.

So the struggle now is to discover some new meaning as well as direction. *Relearning never truly ends.* It's a continuing journey, as it should be, whether grief occurs or not. It's a process of creating new meaning to the past, present and future. In so doing the person is able to make sense of life, including the losses.[12]

As we live, we establish, broaden, enrich, combine, transform, and at times discard or abandon practical involvements with things, places, other persons, and projects. We develop and achieve individual character through our patterns of caring and through the variety, breadth, and depth of our attachments to the surrounding world. Our life histories unfold as we weave and reweave these threads of attachment. Bereavement rends, and sometimes threatens to completely unravel, the fabric of our caring involvement in the world. As we grieve, we struggle to reweave the fabric and establish a new integrity in our pattern of caring involvement.[13]

What is the journey of relearning grief really like? What might we see in a griever's life? Consider this description, which is all too familiar. This is about the journey of *relearning*.

Prior to the death, life was "normal" for all. The world was understandable and familiar. Most go through life with the naïve assumption that what they may desire is possible and conceivable. With the death, the lives of the survivors and their families

70

cease to be "normal." The previous naïve assumptions and "working models" of their lives are no longer valid.

Notification about the death with the social mourning rituals associated with wakes, memorial services, and burial serve as external validation that the person is, indeed, dead. After the initial shock and numbness of knowing the person is dead and going through the public rituals surrounding death, the bereaved begins to learn the meaning of the physical absence (lack of proximity) of the deceased. There is a realization that their world is broken—nothing is as it was before.

Life becomes torn apart for the bereaved. The world no longer has plan, order or direction. Many are encompassed by hopelessness. Some feel powerless to help themselves. Some have a profound state of loneliness in that they feel no one can help or understand them. Their grief also has physical, social, psychological, and cognitive dimensions.

At their lowest point of grief (when grief is the most intense), the bereaved who becomes a resilient survivor experiences a turning point. They come to two simultaneous realizations. One is that the deceased will never, ever return. The other realization is that they must somehow actually "take hold" of their lives. This realization is associated with the bereaved beginning to learn to let go of the pain of grief and beginning to regain a sense of hope for the future. Their grief begins to diminish as they engage in the process of rebuilding their lives and creating a revised model of the world based on a new reality and normality.[14]

It's forever. When a family member dies, life changes forever. As you work with family members of the deceased, you may see different responses and patterns begin to emerge, or you may wonder if these patterns simply aren't being expressed.

One pattern is that of *regret*.

Whether the griever is a child, an adolescent, an adult, parent or sibling, they may feel sorry for the way they treated the other person and wish they had been different. Even if there were some negative patterns associated with the deceased, these, too, are missed. You may hear statements such as the following, "Even when he and I didn't get along, and I swore at him and said I wish he wasn't part of our family, it wasn't true. I didn't really mean that. I wish I'd never said that."

"I was mean at times. There's no other way to describe me. Now I feel terrible. I would like to hear her say, 'It's all right. I forgive you. I love you,' but it won't happen. I miss her now."

"It's not that I said or did bad things to him. I was more neutral. I didn't say the good things. I didn't thank him for all he did. I took him for granted."

If you don't hear regret voiced when you are counseling, ask if the person would like some help in identifying that feeling. You could accomplish this verbally or in having the person write the statement "I regret . . ." and then fill in the details.

Suggestions to Get Past the Regrets

Often when a loved one dies, those who remain wish they had related differently with the person, in some way. When you've helped the counselee identify the regrets, you could ask, "What do you feel good about in your relationship? What do you think _____ was pleased about or was appreciative of in the way you treated him/her? What could you do about your regrets at this time to relinquish them?"

You could also suggest writing a letter of apology to the deceased and reading it at the gravesite or in a room at home. He or she will never hear the words, "I forgive you" from the person who is deceased, but he or she can read in the Scriptures how God forgives them as well as hear their own voice saying that they are forgiven.

A second pattern is the attempt to *understand* or *make sense of the death*. The younger the person or the more violent the circumstances or degree of suddenness all add to the intensity of the response. The questions of "how?" and "why?" are the most common.

There may be a sense of disbelief that causes the person to see everything as if he or she is looking through a veil or a gauze curtain. Nothing is sharp or in focus. The question "Why?" is asked countless times a day. This may be shouted and emphasized with a shaking fist. The person may wonder, *Do I have the right to ask why?* Or wonder if God will be upset if he/she questions what happened.

It's human to ask. Job asked this question 16 times. "Why?" is not just a question—it's also a heart-wrenching cry of protest, of pain. It means "No! This shouldn't be! It isn't right!" "Why?" says, "I need some explanations. I need some answers." Receiving no answer feeds anger. This brings up a side question to this issue. Would any answer suffice at this time? Is there any answer that would ease the person's heart? More than likely the answer is, "No, not really." Answers don't make pain go away.

You may hear the person say:

- "How can something like this happen? It just doesn't make sense to me."
- "I've got to know why. Isn't there someone who can give me an answer?"
- "What were you thinking of when you went on that river rafting trip? You can't swim, and no life vest!"
- "I have so many *whys*, and I'm afraid that there will be no answer . . . ever."

Validate these questions when you counsel. You can't answer them but you can help the one who grieves express them. If you don't hear any of these questions, you could say, "When a death occurs for any reason, often we have questions in our mind. I wonder if you have any questions that you'd like answered."

There is a third grief-processing pattern, which is *reaffirmation*. Many want to affirm the fact that theirs was a positive relationship with the deceased. They may talk about the quality relationship they had or their love for the person or how he or she influenced them or how much they miss the person. It's almost like a declaration for themselves and the world. Here are some possible ways of expressing these longings:

- "I would tell her again and again how much she had an impact on my life."
- "I wish I could sit at his feet again. I wouldn't talk but just enjoy his presence and his pipe smoke."
- "Every day I wake up and miss her. I'd like to see her walk through the house again. I'd even like to hear her nag me again about my eating. I knew she cared, and it was comfortable."
- "I miss hearing her call my name."
- "I miss the sound of his laugh."
- "I miss the fact that she never met my husband."
- "I miss that he never walked me down the aisle."
- "I miss the long talks we used to have."
- "I miss her now, but I'll see her in heaven."

A fourth pattern is *influence*. We are influenced by every person we've ever had a relationship with, and we become so much more aware of this after a death. It's helpful to see and express who we are because of someone else. Sometimes a person is still influenced by the departed's dreams or expectations for them. This could be healthy or unhealthy. Becoming aware of the influence seems to deepen the connection they have with the deceased.

One woman said, "My father died of cancer when I was eight years old, leaving my mother at the age of 29 with two children, several years of college education ahead, little money and few marketable skills. No doubt my lifelong professional interest in helping children, especially those suffering loss and separation, has its roots in my own continued mourning for my father and in my compassion for my mother's gallant struggles to protect my younger brother and me from the economic and personal hardships she faced daily." These are the types of comments you may hear that express the influence of a deceased love one:

- "He may be gone, but I still feel his influence when I make decisions. I get confidence from that."
- "I have a lot of questions I'd like to ask him again."
- "I have questions about heaven. I wish I could ask her some questions up there."

Some influences may be negative but still dominate the survivor's life. Memory work is an important step in the grief process. Here are some memory responses from those who had unfinished business with the deceased:

- "You weren't there for me when I needed you. You turned your back on me when I got pregnant, and I felt so alone."
- "I never saw you when you weren't angry or didn't have a beer in your hand."
- "You controlled Mother and us so much we couldn't breathe."
- "If we could have talked more I could have learned so much about you, and you could have really known me. I think you would have liked me."
- "I wish you would have been nicer to my baby and me."
- "I wish you had been more strict with me. You left it all up to Mom, and she couldn't handle me. I needed your firm hand."
- "I needed you at my recitals, my birthdays, my games. Were you really always at work, or elsewhere?"
- "I have pictures of you, but I don't have your voice. I wish we could have talked."

Memory Work Questions

1. In what way did _____ shape or influence your life?

2. What do you wish _____ would have done to impact your life more?

3. How are you like _____, and how are you unlike this person?

4. What would you like to say to _____ for how he (she) influenced your life?

5. What is the unfinished business that might exist between you and _____ at this time? What could you do about it now?

A final pattern that is important for believers is the reunion in heaven with a spouse, parent, child or sibling—"our relationship is not over but just changed at this time for a while."[15]

- "He's just getting there sooner than I will. I'm looking forward to that time."
- "He's dead, yes, but more alive than I am. Someday we'll reconnect."

There are several questions you can ask now:

- What does the future look like for you at this time?
- Now that _____ has died, what are your hopes for him and you?
- What is the dream for your life and _____ in the future?

The questions in each of the sections of this chapter pertain to issues the one who has lost a loved one will have to face in order to move forward in the midst of grief and relearn life. It is our task then to lead with care and sensitivity and compassion so that the griever can face these issues and resolve them.

Fran

Fran: It may sound silly to some people. I live alone, and I have a dog that is 15 years and 3 months. She's like a kid to me. I am really struggling with knowing when it is the time to let her go. People tell me that I will know when it's time. In fact, I've been up to the vet twice, thinking it's time, and she rallied. So I'm dealing with the anticipatory grief. [She pauses to compose herself.] It weighs very heavily on me that I'll have to do this, because she means so much to me.

Counselor: It's going to be a big loss, isn't it? Tell me about your dog; what is her name?

Fran: Julie Jan. I call her JJ for short. She's a Springer Spaniel. I adopted her in 2001 from a Springer Rescue. I've been in touch with her first mom over the years. When I was hospitalized for depression, and when I came out, she was there. She was the only one. The second time I was hospitalized and I knew I'd need to go back to the hospital, I called the vet and asked if they could board her for a few days. I took her there, went out to the car and took an overdose. Then I went back in the hospital again. She sleeps with me. I'm losing little bits of her along the way. When she lost her hearing, she lost interest in squeaky toys anymore. And now she's lost all of her sassiness. She just stole my heart.

Counselor: And you're seeing her gradually leave you.

Fran: [having a hard time talking and nodding] Yes, it's hard.

Counselor: You're struggling with "I don't want to lose her, but I don't want to see her in pain." And the decisions, you're wondering when will be the right time?

Fran: She doesn't seem to be in pain. She just sleeps a lot. I have been giving her supplements and fluids every day to keep

Helping Those in Grief

her hydrated. I took her to the vet the other day because I was worrying it might hurt for her to eat. I got her in there, and when the vet tried to look at her mouth, she clamped down on her hands. [laughing at the memory] When the vet looked at her gums, she said, "You know, she really doesn't look that bad."

Counselor: Who do you have in your life that understands the love you have for JJ, and the connection?

Fran: I have my mom. My mom might understand. She lives in Florida.

Counselor: Who is there for you right around here?

Fran: [thinking] I just don't know. I think, well, I'm in touch with JJ's first mom, so I know she gets it.

Counselor: What I'm looking for is, is there someone who can go with you when you have to take her in, so you don't have to go alone?

Fran: I thought about that yesterday. I really don't know.

Counselor: What if someone from church or class volunteered and said, "When it's time, call me and I'll go with you"?

Fran: It would be terrific.

Counselor: When JJ is gone, what do you want to do?

Fran: Probably have a funeral. [tears]

Counselor: I'm feeling your loss.

Fran: Most of the time I dissociate as much as possible . . . And then there are times when it seems like it's right now that she's not there. She went to the vet a couple of weeks ago and had to spend the night, and that night I thought, *This is what it will be like when she's gone.*

Counselor: There will be that empty spot for a while. Do you have a job?

Fran: Oh, yeah.

Counselor: Will the people you work with understand?

Fran: Some of them.

Counselor: Maybe when this occurs you could compose a letter to let them know what has happened. You could state how hard this has been for you and how sad you are. When you hear their lack of understanding, you could hand them a letter and say, "Here, I just wanted to update you on what's going on." I think they will appreciate that.

Fran: Yes, I know they're not going to understand.

Counselor: Unless they're dog people, and then they'll think, *She loves her dog.*

Fran: Yes.

Counselor: That would be something to do. Even now you could be saying your goodbyes.

Fran: [struggles to gain composure]

Counselor: Look for people who would walk with you, because it's going to be difficult. This is just as important as the loss of a person.

Fran: Thank you, thank you.

Analysis

This case was a brief interaction that focused on what I felt were Fran's concerns and I attempted to reflect the key issues she was expressing. Some of the questions were designed to help her handle the inevitable and think through the impact as well as diminish the effects of the loss. Validating the significance of the loss of an animal is important. Help the person identify his or her support system as well as ways to engage them as support.

5

The Variations and Complications of Grief

Patterns of Grief

Patterns are found in every part of life. But did you know there are also patterns of ways to grieve, depending on a person's particular personality style? These patterns reflect what a person is experiencing internally as well as his or her outward expression.

There are different types of grievers who follow different patterns of processing grief. There are *intuitive* grievers, whose energy and expression go into their feelings and much less into the cognitive or thinking arena. Grief for the intuitive individual is made up of feelings, painful feelings, and the expression of these is usually through crying.

There are *instrumental* grievers who take the energy from grief and go into the thinking arena rather than feelings. It's more of an intellectual experience. This person looks for activities to deal with what he or she is experiencing.

Both styles are an attempt to deal with loss.

It's rare to find a person who is purely intuitive or purely instrumental. Most people are a mixture of both. They express their grief in a way that reflects both patterns but tend to go toward one end of the continuum or the other. Most people are fairly consistent in the way they handle their grief. Our task as counselors is to help those who grieve to discover ways to express their grief according to their dominant pattern as well as their non-dominant pattern. The authors of *Men Don't Cry . . . Women Do* said:

> Intuitive grievers experience their losses deeply. Feelings are varied and intense and loosely follow the descriptions of acute grief that have been cited so frequently in the literature (see, for example, Lindemann, 1944). Emotions vary, ranging from shock and disbelief to overwhelming sorrow and a sense of loss or self-control. The intuitive griever may experience grief as a series or waves of acutely painful feelings. Intuitive grievers often find themselves without energy and motivation. Their expressions of grief truly mirror their inner experiences. Anguish and tears are almost constant companions.
>
> Intuitive grievers gain strength and solace from openly sharing their inner experiences with others—especially other grievers. Some intuitive grievers are very selective about their confidants and, consequently may not seek help from a larger group. Others seek out larger groups, especially those with similar types of losses. For intuitive grievers, a grief expressed is a grief experienced (or a burden shared is half a burden). Because openly expressing and sharing feelings is traditionally identified as a female brain, intuitive grieving is usually associated with women. Of course, this is not always the case; male intuitive grievers grieve in ways similar to female grievers.[1]

Keep in mind the two main factors of the different patterns—how the person experiences grief and how he or she expresses grief. Some of the couples I've counseled contained both patterns. A couple in their late fifties came after the suicide death of their 35-year-old son. The husband looked at the situation in an extreme instrumental manner and said, "Well, what happened, happened. We can't change anything. We just have to go on." He returned to work the next day and rarely talked about how he was doing. His wife was just the opposite, so both ended up grieving alone. For grief to be real to an intuitive, it needs to be talked about with others and often. The tears are not just frequent but can range from sobbing to wailing. The duration of their grief expression is often a factor as well. They tend to seek out others with similar experiences. For some, their entire life for a while centers around their grief experience.

Because intuitive grievers are not dealing as much with the cognitive response to their grief, some of the grief symptoms may last longer, taking the form of confusion, an inability to concentrate, disorientation and disorganization. They may have a greater struggle handling tasks in the thinking area.

As you meet with those in grief, discovering their grieving pattern is paramount to helping them. Connecting with an intuitive griever works by reflecting what you're hearing or sensing they may be experiencing. Remember, however, that most are not totally intuitive, so don't neglect the thinking side of their grief. This person may need more assistance from you with planning and structuring his or her life. Moving the person to his or her least dominant side can be helpful in finding balance.

Questions for the Intuitive Griever

1. I'd like to hear about the time when expressing your feelings is the most helpful and when it's the least.
2. When others respond to you when you're upset, what is the best way for them to respond? How would they know this?
3. What could we do to think through some steps that could help you this week?
4. You've said you're getting tired of living in your feelings and crying so much. What do you think could be done to make some changes?

When you minister to the instrumental griever, remember that they are primarily responding from the left side of their brain. They tend to perceive their loss differently than the intuitive person. They may respond initially to thoughts explaining what has happened rather than feelings about the event. They tend to feel more of a sense of control, more of "I can handle this." They are quite bothered if their grief disrupts left-brain functioning with confusion, forgetting, difficulty concentrating, and so on. They do respond with feelings, but not as intensely. As Martin and Doka have said, "For the intuitive griever, feelings are intense 'colors,' whereas for the instrumental griever they are 'pastels.' "[2]

Instrumental grievers are seen as those who do not cry or seek help from others. Their way of dealing with their grief is action, and often it is planned action rather than random. Sometimes what they engage in is "mindless" activity, but it keeps them busy. Other activities could be a way of directly expressing their grief or memorializing the deceased, such as planting a tree or carving a wooden headstone. Activities are an attempt to bring things back to normal and create a new sense of security.[3]

Questions for the Instrumental Griever

1. Let's talk about what you've done since the death of _____ _____ and how this has impacted you.
2. What do you think you could do now that would be beneficial for you?
3. If someone asked you to describe your feelings over the loss, what would you say?
4. What emotions would you like to be able to express, and what makes it difficult?

The third pattern is *blended*—a strong presence of both the intuitive and the instrumental.

Sometimes what we see in a person is not who they really are. Sometimes other factors cause them to respond in an opposite way to who they really are. For example, the intuitive griever who feels he needs to be strong and in charge for the rest of the family may, when alone, engage in uncontrollable weeping.

When you are counseling, listen to the person's language. Listen for feeling words or thinking words. Validate the way in which he or she responds and processes grief. Encourage the person to consider responding in his or her less dominant pattern. Above all, use the person's preferred language. If they're using cognitive or factual words, do the same. If they're using feeling words, then that's your language too.

Honor the person's way of thinking and speaking. The more similar you appear to the counselee, the greater comfort he or she will experience. Dr. Linda Schupp described it this way: "Commonalities create comment. Differences produce distance."

There has always been a debate about gender differences actually existing. Looking at intuitive vs. instrumental is a more accurate way of distinguishing differences. Gender does influence patterns of grieving, but it doesn't determine it. Personality distinctions and differences come into play as well.

Having looked at these patterns, imagine that you are going to see a family of six—whose youngest member was just killed. Here are the remaining family members and their grieving patterns:

- **Father**—Instrumental—fairly dominant, outgoing, salesman, leader type
- **Mother**—Strong intuitive—Introverted, very involved mother, conflict avoider, passive
- **17-year-old son**—Extroverted, some ADD tendencies, sports fanatic, intuitive, very close to deceased
- **15-year-old son**—just like the father
- **11-year-old daughter**—Intuitive, didn't get along with the deceased, more of the scapegoat
- **10-year-old daughter**—Intuitive, loner, doesn't like her dad, tolerates siblings, loved the deceased

How would you minister to each one? Do you keep them together? Separate them? What will impede the grieving pattern for each one? What are your goals for the counseling session? After you have completed this book, return to these questions and formulate your answers.

In your counseling experiences, you will encounter a variation of grief called *complicated mourning*.

What Is Complicated Mourning?

"I'm stuck. I don't seem to be able to get anywhere. I just had the one-year anniversary of Bill's death, and I look back and don't see that I'm any different than the first week after he died. I've turned into an over-reactor. I hear about any loss and I come apart. I think of death a lot—my parents', my daughter's, my own. When it comes to others, where are they? They're not here, or at least they don't stick around. Don't ask me 'How do you feel?' because I don't. I don't want to—it hurts."

Where would you begin with this person? What has she told you? Aside from the specifics, she is saying, "I have a case of complicated grieving." There are a number of indicators, and you need to be aware of these, for they will need your attention. You can attribute some complications to personality, past issues and so on, and tend to overlook them. When you see several of these, look at them as a cluster of symptoms. The message is "complicated."

The following characteristics are an accurate profile of the complicated griever. Each characteristic will have a sample question you may want to use with the person you are counseling.

1. No matter what other type of loss is encountered there is a heightened sensitivity or an overreaction to it. This may be just an inner response or it may be obvious to others.

   Question: Are there times when you surprise yourself by your response to other losses?

2. There is a pervasive anxiety over the possible dying of others, such as friends or family members, as well as the fear that they too may die.

   Question: To what extent do you think about the deaths of others or yourself?

3. There is a continuous and persistent realization of the deceased and their relationship.

   Question: How would _____ have described your relationship? Or tell me about a difficult time you experienced in your relationship.

4. There is an apparent inability to relax. The person seems tense or wired, constantly on the go, almost driven.

   Question: If you sat down and did nothing, how would you feel? What would that say about you?

5. The way in which the person behaves is compulsive; seems rigid with very little flexibility. Some behaviors seem ritualistic in nature.

   Question: How do you handle change or even a surprise at this time?

6. The person's thinking is constantly focused on loss and could appear to be overly preoccupied with the event.

   Question: To what extent or how much time do you dwell on loss, and what is the effect of this on your life?

7. The emotions are there but there is an inability to experience them. They've been blocked but still exist under the surface. The person may or may not be aware of their existence. Some will feel numb while others will feel as if they're going to explode.

   Question: What emotions aren't you experiencing but you're aware they still exist?

8. Some have an inability to even talk about their loss. They avoid or resist the discussion or change the subject even

though there are issues that need to be discussed. It's the same for thoughts or feelings.

Question: What do you think is making it difficult for you to talk about your loss? If for some reason you were to talk about your loss, what part would you talk about?

9. There's an inability to experience loving feelings, which is part of the blockage process. The person's love feelings for others may be dreaded, or they can't respond to others' love.

Question: Can you describe the last time you've experienced love, either giving or receiving, and what that was like?

10. Relationships with others are marred or disrupted. The person may avoid others or live in fear. It's risky to love—he or she may lose the person or experience hurt again.

Question: Describe your love relationship at the present time and what fears you may have.

11. In a way, the person may become his or her own enemy when it comes to building healthy relationships. He or she may behave in a way that eventually destroys the relationship—or may move into relationships too soon. The person could be driven to help others without allowing others to reach out to them.

Question: What have you learned about relationships at this time that you wish you'd known before?

12. Substance abuse may be employed on an increased level to control feelings.

Question: Compared to three months ago, how would you compare your use of medication?

13. There are constant feelings of isolation and alienation from others that feed the feelings of loneliness. Unfortunately, much of the time it's self-created and creates a vicious cycle.

    Question: When do you feel the closest to others and when do you feel isolated?

14. There are tense emotions that can cripple relationships and push others away. The person continues on and on—irritability, anger, a belligerent attitude, little patience and tolerance for others as well as depression.

    Question: Often in grief we experience an increase of anger or irritability. We have little patience and tolerance of others. To what extent have you experienced any of this?

15. Crying goes on and on. It can be continuous, with only limited ability to contain or control it.

    Question: Describe your crying and what you think this is saying.[4]

You may prefer to deal with certainty rather than uncertainty, in your own life as well as in your counselees. But many of those in grief will have difficulty dealing with their grief because of the uncertainty associated with its presence. What adds to the dilemma of handling uncertainty is that there is not a right way or particular way to cope with uncertainty. This description of complicated loss was given in the book *Ambiguous Loss*:

There are two basic kinds of ambiguous loss. In the first type, people are perceived by family members as physically absent but psychologically present, because it's unclear if they are dead or alive. When nothing is available, there is no closure.

In the second type of ambiguous loss, a person is perceived as physically present but psychologically absent. This condition is illustrated in the extreme by people with Alzheimer's disease, addictions and other chronic mental illnesses.

Of all the losses experienced in personal relationships, ambiguous loss is the most devastating, because it remains unclear and indeterminate.

Perceiving loved ones as present when they are physically gone or perceiving them as gone when they are physically present can make a person feel helpless. It makes them more prone to depression, anxiety and relationship conflicts. It leads to complicated grief. It's not easy for stepchildren to handle a biological parent's being excluded or for a spouse to constantly deal with his or her brain-injured spouse who now functions like a five-year-old.[5]

If you suspect ambiguous loss, ask the counselee the following question: "Have you experienced any kind of loss that doesn't make sense or for which you can't seem to get any closure?"

Ambiguous loss is also a psychologically distressing event that is outside the realm of ordinary human experience; like the events triggering Post-Traumatic Stress Disorder (PTSD), it lacks resolution and traumatizes. With ambiguous loss, the trauma (the ambiguity) continues to exist in the present. It is *not post* anything. Ambiguous loss is typically a long-term situation that traumatizes and immobilizes, not a single event that later has a flashback. But ambiguous loss is unique in that the trauma goes on and on in what families describe as a roller-coaster ride, during which they alternate between hope and hopelessness. A loved one is missing, then sighted, then lost again. Or a family member is dying, then goes into remission, then the illness returns again in full force.[6]

Goodbyes are important in moving forward in grief; but in so many instances in this type of grief there is no goodbye when people leave. Ambiguous loss can also include the losses associated with divorce, adoption, migration and over-commitment to work. In divorce, something is lost—the marriage—but something continues—the parenting. There's a great ambiguity in divorce.

The psychological absence in ambiguous loss can be devastating. Too often there's little support for the losses that are ongoing. So look for these types of losses. To diagnose, you could ask, "Is there something that keeps you from getting the closure you're looking for in his death?" or "What could you do to be able to really say goodbye?"

When loss moves into the arena of being a crisis or a trauma, the impact is so much deeper. Some of the counselees you see will be living with this as their normal life.

Traumatic grief lengthens and multiples every aspect of the grief process. Traumatic grief is a direct response to disastrous events that threaten safety, security and beliefs around which we structure and order our lives. It can happen directly to the person or to a family member.

Certain events are more likely to precipitate traumatic grief reactions and share some common themes. Here is a list of descriptors that identify what can bring on traumatic grief reactions:

- **Unexpected**—The surprise elements stun and shock. We feel dazed and disoriented.
- **Uncontrollable**—The event is beyond our abilities to change it. We feel powerless and vulnerable.
- **Unimaginable**—The horrific elements are not familiar to our way of life. Our frame of reference does not include what we are witnessing. We feel appalled and horrified.
- **Unreal**—The event is too strange to process. We see but do not comprehend what we are seeing. We feel confused and disoriented.
- **Unfair**—We feel like victims who have done nothing to deserve this tragedy. We feel hurt, puzzled, angry or fearful.
- **Unforgivable**—We need to blame someone or something. What do we do with our anger, rage and urge to punish? We feel powerless.
- **Unprecedented**—Nothing like this has happened before. We don't have a script to follow. We feel directionless.
- **Unprepared**—We haven't perceived a reason to ready ourselves for an unimaginable catastrophe. Our defense mechanisms may be inadequate to handle the demand. We feel overwhelmed.

- **Uncertainty**—We don't fully know the long-range effect on our-selves, our families, our jobs, our future and the future of our offspring. We feel ambivalent and torn between hope and fear.[7]

To assist you in ministering to the grieving individual, use the fol-lowing questions. These questions can be discussed together or you could ask the counselee to complete them in writing.

1. Tell me about the death and what led up to it. If _____ _____'s death followed an illness, please answer the following:

   - What was _____'s experience during his/her illness?
   - What was your experience during _____'s illness?
   - What was the length and course of the illness?
   - What, if any, was the nature of your participation in _____'s care during the illness?
   - Did you ever discuss _____'s death with him/her? If so, what was this like?
   - What, if anything, was the nature of your anticipatory grief during _____'s illness?
   - What were the hardest parts for you in _____ _____'s illness?
   - Do you have any unfinished business or unresolved conflicts about anything that happened or didn't hap-pen during _____'s illness? If so, please explain.
   - What would you change, if anything, if you could about the illness experience for you? For _____ _____?
   - Were you prepared when _____ _____ died?

- How could things have been better for you during
  _____'s illness? At his/her death?
- What, if anything, do you feel good about regarding
  your interaction with _____ during
  his/her illness?

2. What happened immediately after the death and in the few
   days thereafter?
3. Tell me about _____. What type of relationship did the two of you have?
4. You've told me a great deal about what was positive in the
   relationship. Could you tell me a little about the aspects that
   were not so positive?
5. Exactly what did _____ and the
   relationship with him/her mean to you and give to you in
   your life?
6. In what ways (positive and negative) did _____
   _____ help you or cause you to be the person you
   are/were?
7. Specifically, what have you lost in your life with _____
   _____'s death?
8. Do you have any unfinished business with _____
   _____? Anything you would have wanted to say
   or do that would have made you more comfortable with ending the relationship, but you never said or did, and therefore
   lack closure?
9. What do you think you need to do to finish this business?
10. Please describe for me the various reactions you have had
    since _____'s death.

- What specific kinds of responses did you have, and what
  particular kinds of behaviors did you witness in yourself?
- Did you have any reactions and/or behaviors that were
  unexpected or that frightened you? If so, what were they?

11. Tell me what you have done to cope with _____
    _____'s death.

12. How would you complete these sentences?

    • The things I do/did that help/helped me the most are/
    were . . .
    • If I have/had problems related to this loss, they seem/
    seemed to be in the area of . . .
    • The most difficult parts of this for me are/have been . . .
    • My most major concerns in all of this are . . .
    • What I have specifically done to try to help myself is . . .

13. How have others reacted to _____'s death?

14. Have your relationships with others changed since _____
    _____'s death?

15. What types of support have you received from others to help
    you cope with _____'s death?

16. Were there any types of support or recognition you required
    but did not receive, or any specific persons from whom you
    needed support or recognition but did not receive it?

17. Please describe what happened to you in the time since
    _____ died. For example, what changes
    (either gains or losses)?

18. In what ways have you been changed by this death?

19. In what ways are you the same as before?

20. Many times after a person loses a loved one, he or she has some
    experiences in which there is a sense of the presence of the loved
    one. Sometimes the mourner takes these experiences as a "sign"
    or as some form of communication from the loved one. Some-
    times there are vivid dreams, or the mourner has an experience
    of seeing the image of the deceased or hearing that person's
    voice. Sometimes mourners are reluctant to talk about this be-
    cause they think it makes them sound crazy, even though they
    are not. I know that this happens with many mourners, and I
    am wondering if anything like this has ever happened to you.

• Have you ever had any of these types of experiences or anything like them?
• What was it like for you to have this happen?
• How did you respond?

21. How are you choosing to deal with _____
_____'s room? Clothing? Other possessions?
What is this like for you?

• Have you saved any special items?
• What do you do with it/them?
• Where do you keep it/them?
• What made you choose it/them?
• How does/do it/they represent you?
• What does/do it/they make you feel when you encounter it/them?

22. At this point, how is it for you when you come across things that remind you of _____ or bring back memories of him/her? For example, how may you react when you see pictures of him/her, suddenly remember a special time you shared or go to an event and wish he/she would be there with you, such as a wedding or holiday gathering?

23. How do you think you will ultimately do in your grief and mourning, and in learning to live without _____
_____?

24. What remains for you to do or change in your grief and mourning and in your life to reach the point where you will be doing the best you can in coping with this loss and living without _____?[8]

In your counseling, you will encounter numerous losses that not only do not involve death but that society may not recognize as losses and fail to support the grievers. Every culture has its own set of norms or rules. Dr. Kenneth Doka described it this way:

Yet individuals experience a range of losses that are not death related. Divorce, relocation, the relinquishment of a child for adoption or foster care, the loss of a job, or incarceration are all examples of non-death-related losses that can be significant separations arousing grief. In addition, humans form attachments with a wide range of individuals—friends, coworkers, clergy, coaches, therapists, Even possessions can take on great significance and meaning in our lives. We may grieve the loss of property in a robbery, fire, flood or other circumstance, especially if the property has great sentimental or monetary value.[9]

Unfortunately, many losses are not socially defined as significant. Secondary losses may fall into this category. You as a counselor can expect to be exposed more and more to disenfranchised grief. Throughout this book you are asked to think and interact with numerous cases to build your insights and skills for various types of grief situations you might encounter. Let's now move to a discussion of the recovery stage for complicated grief.

Healing Complicated Grief

When working with someone who is experiencing complicated grief, what is the best way to help this person? You will need to create the best way to draw upon everything you have learned about this type of grief, about its impact and how to tailor your response to the uniqueness of the griever. Sometimes you can craft an approach on the spot, which is my style, or just rely on what you have learned and your years of experience. But the most important strategy is to rely on your teacher, the Holy Spirit, who will give you the insight, direction and words to share. The Holy Spirit must be at work within us as counselors, and within the grieving person, to successfully begin the healing process.

There are times when I have no idea where to go or what to say, and I cannot rely upon myself. Remember, when we sit with those in grief, we have been given the privilege of ministering to someone at probably one of the most vulnerable times of his or her life. We need to ask for the wisdom and guidance of the Holy Spirit and ask Him to bring our prayers to the Father, for there are times when we need to pray, want to pray, but are unable to do so adequately.

Having stated the foundation for what we do, you may find some of these suggestions and guidelines similar to and overlapping some of what I've said about trauma treatment in my handbook *The Complete Guide to Crisis and Trauma Counseling*. That's probably true, but there will be additional guidelines as well.

My first step with a counselee in moving forward after building a relationship and helping to normalize and educate is to hear the person's story again and again. Part of our task as counselors is to help the counselee face the details of the event so that we can help them look at the event several times from various angles. It may sound as if we're over-leading the griever by this approach, but this is a necessary step in their healing.

A mother came in for her eighth session of counseling. Her 36-year-old son had taken his life. When she sat down, she began to share again the events of the last week of his life, not only from her perspective but from his wife's and his two brothers'. My role was that of an attentive listener, for she needed to tell her story again and again. It was her way of trying to make sense of what doesn't make sense. Remember that most people are constantly telling their story, but in their head, which doesn't move them toward healing.

You can help the person review the event, which could involve reconstructing the details; and, yes, they will experience it all over again, but by doing so the event will lose its dominating power. It's safer for the person to discharge the emotional material in your presence than repeating it in his or her head. Telling the detailed story again and again, in one session, can be beneficial. Sometimes I ask, "If a bystander were there and told the story from their perspective, what would it sound like?"

The author of *Crisis Counseling and Therapy* says:

> The role of the clinician is to facilitate the storytelling and sharing in such a way as to progressively bring more of the details of the experience to light.

The storytelling process may be repeated numerous times as the victims search for ways to integrate experience that has no place in current functioning. One therapist explained it this way: "It is like an old-fashioned flour sifter. To get the flour to the right consistency, you have to turn the sifter over and over and over until it eventually is all sifted through." In telling the story, the crisis client gradually incorporates an alien experience into consciousness. One client said descriptively, "I felt a little stupid, but I needed to tell every detail of the accident over and over again before I could really begin to figure out what to do. Telling it over and over I finally 'heard' what I had to say. What was outside of me finally got in."

Successfully facilitating this step of the model requires the therapist to be skilled at listening, encouraging, summarizing and questioning. Questioning is purposefully placed last in this order. The use of questions is likely to distract the storyteller. Reflecting phrases or themes is a much more effective strategy, assisting the speaker to recount important details of the crisis event. Adequate time should be invested so that this step of the model maximizes its benefits. The power and importance of telling the story not only begins the healing process: It *is* the healing process.[10]

This repeating process uses what is called *unlayering* or *unlocking* to allow the person to view the event respectively, thus peeling off layers of thoughts and emotions, opinions and even desires. Each time the situation is looked at, questions are either answered or the need to answer them diminishes. One of the most helpful approaches I've discovered is repetitious handwriting of the event in as much detail as possible. The use of the hand in this can drain off emotion and energy that no other way seems to do. It can be exhausting, which is beneficial. It takes time, and some may delay the process, but it gets thoughts and intrusive memories out and diminishes their frequency and intensity.

We remember interrupted tasks until they are completed. Once resolved, we cease thinking about them. That is, understanding, seeing clearly, sorting out or organizing our thoughts settles issues. It appears that different aspects of a memory are stored in different parts of the brain. Language appears to unify the diverse elements of experience. Writing increases our focus and understanding. Putting a complex issue into words helps us organize it, understand it and then remember it with less stress. Once we have done the work of sorting out what needs to be done and put it on paper in a clear, meaningful way, the mind relaxes without swirling confusion. So writing helps bring order, detachment and meaning. And because writing is slower than talking, it promotes more detailed thought. One author said, "A pattern emerges. The goal is flexible engagement. That is, we willingly face the pain as needful. We face the worst and see it clearly, without fear. Sometimes we see a way to improve upon the worst. Sometimes we see a new way to interpret the event. Sometimes we simply accept life with more peace and understanding."[11]

Sometimes the counselee will read his or her writing aloud or just leave it. Sometimes I ask the person to rate the level of his or her emotional upset on a scale of 0 to 10 immediately after writing.

The following four numbered items are actual statements from several counseling sessions. Some are the opening remarks. I would like you to (1) identify the main issues, (2) identify any feelings expressed, and (3) write out your verbal responses to what was said. Later in this book you will find these remarks as part of a verbatim counseling session with either my own or others' responses.

1. **Diane**: My husband died, and he has done pretty much about everything in the home all of our lives. I'm having to make decisions I didn't use to have to make. I have children who are acting up, in-laws who all of a sudden want to be in

control of my decisions, wanting to make decisions that should be my decisions. I'm nervous about the consequences that could happen later on if I make a decision they don't like. My parents are calling about the grandkids. I am so overwhelmed that I don't know what to do. I don't even know where to start.

2. **Diane**: I feel lost and alone. I'm trying to figure out where God is right now. I believe in God, I'm just not sure where He is. I feel like He needs to give me an answer and tell me where to go right now so I could know what to do. I feel lost right now. I don't even know how to do the simple things in life. When I get up, I don't even know what to do, the first thing to do.

3. **Carol**: My oldest adopted child is now living in a placement home out of state. One of the big losses is that I can't stop grieving *his* losses. He was abandoned at seven months and left in a crib until he was six years old. He just got out of diapers at 17. I think I'm grieving my kid's losses. I just found out about a significant sexual abuse incident with my younger son in an orphanage, which he's been carrying around, and I'm just trying to make up for what they both missed. I'm not able to and I'm feeling hopeless. Before Jimmy was taken out of state he became very violent. He broke up the house. And in the middle of all that I found out that my new husband had been lying to me and I couldn't trust him anymore. I'm not sure where I am in the grieving process. I'm doing a lot of work. I'm trying to process all this. I'm wondering who I can trust. My trust has been shattered. This is on top of feeling responsible for my sons. And my oldest son is now in the care of other people. It's hard to have your child being cared for in out-of-home care, and it's hard because you're not sure if they're going to be abused again. My youngest son, who is blind, told me about this abuse right before I put him on a

bus to go to a boarding school. So they are both being cared for by other people that I don't necessarily trust. So I'm really feeling hopeless.

4. **W:** Norm, I came in because I've really been struggling with depression for the last couple of months. I felt like I made some mistakes when my loved one died. I just really knew he was getting sicker and sicker, and I felt like I should do something about it. At the time, I just kept thinking he needs rest and his body needs to recoup. If I had taken him in earlier he might still be with me. I don't know quite how to get rid of the guilt I've been feeling. I keep blaming myself for his death.

The following is a case similar to one you may encounter, as unusual as it seems. Mrs. M was 47 and had been divorced for seven years. All three children were still at home, but the oldest was to be married within a month. A month ago, her ex-husband died in an automobile accident, leaving a wife and two small children. He lived 50 miles away in another city.

Mrs. M: I never thought I'd be sitting here talking about this. It never crossed my mind that I'd have to go through this type of experience. I thought all this pain was over. It's been such a shock. Ed was only 48. He was healthy and then to die like that. You know, he left me for the woman he was married to . . . [long pause] I lost him then and I had to work through all that pain . . . that rejection and anger and grief . . . it took so long and now it's like I lost him again. I don't understand my grief. If I were married I could understand, but not this grief. I was over him . . . I thought. I don't know . . . what's going on?

Counselor: It sounds like you're shocked by what you're experiencing. A repeated loss is really confusing.

Mrs. M: It's more than confusing—I understand grief, but I don't understand the intensity of some of my anger—not at him so much as the situation—his relatives, the funeral home and even my friends. It's like I'm not expected to be able to grieve . . . like I shouldn't, because I'm the ex, a non-person. It was so awkward—friends who heard about his death, some called and thought I'd be glad, like he deserved this for what he did. I couldn't believe it. He was still the father of my children.

Counselor: Others didn't understand, and you didn't get the support you were looking for . . . ?

Mrs. M: It's true, but it gets worse than that. The feeling of isolation makes me feel like there is something wrong with me. I'm hurting and grieving, but others would be shocked to know that. His death has resurrected some of our old issues that I thought were over. You know, resolved, but I guess not.

Counselor: Could it be that the healing you believed had occurred wasn't completed?

Mrs. M: I think so . . . unfortunately. [sighs] I'm concerned about the children and the impact on them. He was supposed to be in my daughter's wedding even though we had a lot of conflict over that . . . and he was helping pay for it . . . and now what? One of my sons had a terrible relationship with him and hasn't shed a tear. He just says . . . "whatever" . . . and shows no feelings. My other son was devastated. He loved his dad so much, and even though he had little time with him, when he did it was good for him . . . My daughter is grieving for him and for her wedding and doesn't know if she wants to go forward with the wedding or not. And . . . and . . . I know this sounds selfish in light of him dying in such a way, and so young, but I've got to survive . . . I was getting $1,800 support a month . . . now what? I didn't get it this month and probably won't get any more . . . what will I do? I'm sure she'll get any insurance. I'm stuck, I'm left out, and I hate it that I'm grieving so much for him.

What would *you* say at this point? Before you continue reading, (1) identify the main issues, (2) identify any feelings expressed, and (3) write out your verbal responses to what was said.

The Death of an Ex-Spouse

The impact of the death of an ex-spouse is a situation that occurs more and more in our culture with the rising divorce rate. Sometimes the loss response is minimal for the spouse but monumental for their children together. And if the death occurs before the divorce is resolved there could be many additional issues to address.

Regrets may be intense at this time. Sometimes there is the feeling that the surviving ex-spouse somehow contributed to the death because of the divorce, or the other might be alive had there not been a divorce. When counseling in this situation, there are several factors to consider:

- The person may still have a relationship but he/she is no longer married.
- If the ex is ill or in the hospital, does he/she visit?
- Where does the ex fit at a funeral—is he/she recognized or ignored? What if the ex has remarried? This type of loss is an example of disenfranchised grief. There is little recognition or support for the ex for this loss.

How do you share grief with your ex's new spouse? The ex can't publicly mourn the death without explaining the divorce. Where *do* they fit in? The most critical factor in the recovery is the degree to which the ex-spouse has worked through the previous loss of the divorce. If the death occurs within five years of the divorce, there's a tendency for the ex-spouse's reactions to be more severe. Once again, children could be the forgotten grievers here. What if the divorce was 10 years ago and the ex has moved on, but her children still connect with their father every week? Their grief over his death could be quite intense but with little support or recognition.

Help the grieving person recognize the fact that the death of his or her ex-spouse is a loss. The person may not believe that he or she has a right to grieve. Some of the steps and concerns to address are:

1. Explore the history and nature of their relationship. Look at before, during and after.

2. Look at the person's response to loss at the time of the divorce. You may discover there are still parts of his/her life impacted by the earlier loss, and now you can talk about them.

3. Identify any changes the person has experienced in response to the loss or the expected loss of the ex. Some people may not admit the loss or be aware of their grief. As one ex-wife said, "Grieve? Why should I grieve? I was glad to be out of there when we divorced."

4. Identify and help resolve emotional responses to this loss. Two major responses could be anger and guilt. Some of these responses may stem from the divorce or the divorce process. Sometimes the pain of the process of disillusionment is the worst part. Normalize any ambivalent feelings they may have. Many lack an understanding of what they may feel or are supposed to feel.

Lack of response or compassion to the children's response or too intense a reaction may be quite upsetting to the person. All these are typical as well as understandable. Which person did the "divorcing" will also impact response.

How others grieve and what they say at this time may be a source of discomfort as well.

- "I thought you were rid of him at the divorce. Why the tears?"
- "She never treated you or any husband right. Move on. The kids are."
- "Congratulations! You probably wanted him dead before."

Perhaps it's the counselee's extended family that's grieving intensely, and they are questioning the person's "lack of compassion" for someone who was his/her spouse for 20 years. And don't forget the children; a child may become irate over not being able to attend the funeral.

1. Identify issues or difficulties that emerged during the illness or funeral and explore their impact and how they can be resolved. There may be anger at the funeral director, at ex-in-laws, at medical personnel or hospital staff for policies or remarks that excluded them. As one man said, "No one really encouraged me to grieve or gave me the right to grieve. I felt like a non-person, just in the way."

   Dr. Kenneth Doka suggests, "Because these experiences are not uncommon among ex-spouses, it is worthwhile to trace the client's role and reactions during the illness. (How did the client find out about the illness? Did he or she visit? How was the client treated? What was he or she feeling? What factors led the ex-spouse not to visit?) It is important also to trace the client's roles and reactions at the funeral. (What was he or she feeling? How did the ex-spouse make the decision to attend or not to attend? How did people respond to the ex-spouse's presence? What does he or she remember of the eulogy/homily? How comfortable was the client at the funeral? Did he or she receive time off from work?).[12]

2. If there was any unfinished business, help your counselee develop a way to resolve this by asking,

   • In any way is there something unfinished between the two of you?
   • What would you like to do to resolve this?
   • How can you move forward in your life without this hindering you?
   • How will you respond to _____'s family any differently now?

3. Identify and work on issues such as resolving anger, saying goodbye, asking for or giving forgiveness.

When an ex-spouse dies, it will affect life in many ways, and these need to be identified as well as explored for their long-term effects. One of the major effects could be financial, especially if the deceased was paying spousal and/or child support. The counselee could have been cut off from life insurance or inheritance, which can generate anger and resentment, or could still receive it, which can create guilt. And it's not just what happens to the ex-spouse, but to the children and even the grandchildren.

The ex's own life could change in its routine or contact because of the loss of his/her ex-spouse. Perhaps the two were still working together on childrearing, and that support is no longer there. The children may be cut adrift with the loss, since they can no longer visit on weekends, holidays or summers, and this puts more pressure on the remaining ex. To address these issues, simply ask:

- In what way is your life impacted financially by this death?
- In what way are your children affected financially by this death?
- In what ways will your life will be different because of this loss?[13]

Two possible counseling responses: "It's not just your life that's been disrupted, but everyone's. I sense that you're feeling hopeless about what to do and would like some answers," or "You have a number of concerns, so it may be difficult to know where to begin. Which issue is troubling you the most? Where would you like to begin?"

Let's end this chapter with the words of an adult child's response to his father's death. He was 23 years old and visibly shaken when he came to see me. He had only been married for three weeks, and his father had just died. His parents divorced when he was 13.

J: I don't even know where to start. My mother . . . [pause] she . . . she . . . Well, I guess I'll start with my first loss. When I was young, my parents seemed to fight all the time. It was hard, but you know, I never thought they couldn't work it out. Just weeks after my thirteenth birthday, my dad came in my room one night and told me he was moving out. I could hardly breathe. What would we do without my father? My mother had been angry and it seemed like she was moving on. But me? I just missed my dad. It was so hard only getting to see him once or twice a month. But as I got older, I had a choice, and I chose to spend more time with my dad and his new wife. My mother also remarried, and she seemed to be happy. She had a new baby and everything seemed to fall into place. I fell in love. I guess I said that. I've only been married a short time and was leaving for boot camp in Georgia the next week. I actually was on my way to Georgia, and leaving that day, when my wife came to find me. She told me my dad had a heart attack and died instantly. He was only 56. I always thought he was old, but to die so young. He doesn't seem so old any longer. I came right home and helped my stepmom plan the funeral. I thought I would be okay. But now I just don't know what to say. It was so horrible. My mom . . . well, she insisted on going to his funeral. I wasn't sure if it was a good idea, but like I said, both she and my dad had remarried, and I thought they had moved on. But you would have never known that at the funeral. My mom . . . oh, just picturing it and hearing her is so difficult. She carried on and cried loudly. And when the funeral was over and it was time to say goodbye and walk by his casket, she ran up there and screamed my father's name over and over again. She just kept saying, "I should never have let you go. You were the only one I loved." My father's new wife was there with her family, and I didn't know what to do. You know, I love both my parents, but this just sent me over the edge. All I can think is, "Mom, you let him go. You were happy to see him go. I was the one who was hurting when you and dad divorced." It was so tough when I heard that my father had died, and I still can hardly believe it. But the pain of his death has now been magnified, and I feel like I'm 13 again, sitting in my room by myself, crying because I don't know how I'm going to live without my dad.

Loss upon loss upon loss; there will be many instances in which the person you counsel has experienced multiple losses that all need attention. This is one of the factors that help to create complicated grief. In addition to the complexity of the issues, look for all the forgotten or neglected people connected to a loss, and reach out to them.

6

Handling "Relief" in Grief

The subject of this chapter is not discussed very much, but it needs to be! There is a wide range of emotions experienced by any person dealing with grief, including, for some, a sense of relief. What is the right response, and what is the wrong one? What should or shouldn't be? Sometimes we run into rigid and even misguided ideas about grief. Yes, death can be a change for the worse, but sometimes it could also contain changes for the better.

In the presence of death and its ensuing events, we experience pressure to conform to certain behaviors. Feelings of relief are rarely considered, and criticism is not voiced, no matter how despicable the character of the deceased. Sometimes what is not said is more significant than what is said, but people feel uncomfortable with those who don't "grieve right."

At a service for an older woman who was known to be cantankerous and a generally unpleasant person to be around, whether interacting with family members or friends, the person giving the eulogy shocked everyone with the glowing and positive accolades she spoke about the deceased. Family members gave each other puzzled looks as if to say, "Is she talking about the woman we knew and disliked?" Finally, after enduring a long and fictitious presentation that was a figment of the presenter's imagination, those in the audience finally felt justified. The song that was supposed to be played at this point in the service was

"Somewhere Over the Rainbow"; but someone made a mistake (perhaps intentionally) and in place of the scheduled song the music to "Ding Dong, the Witch Is Dead" came on, much to the delight of family and friends.

Relief isn't only for those who die; it can also come for the person or family that remains.

> While the tremendous relief that occurs after the end of a prolonged illness is partly the result of having grieved the person so intensely prior to death, it may also be facilitated by the emotional detaching that took place then. Family members recognize that the person they loved has been missing from their lives for a long time, and when death comes, it will be welcomed rather than dreaded.[1]

Many believe that it is easier on those remaining when it has been a gradual process of dying as compared to a sudden, tragic death. But research is showing that chronic stressors, such as caregiving or watching a spouse suffer from an ongoing illness, are believed to be more difficult for psychological adjustment than stressors of shorter duration. Who knows for sure? Either way, it is painful. Grievers can experience both tremendous pain and tremendous relief at the same time.[2]

You may also run into cases of "relationship relief." This is where the one who died was a constant source of criticism, abuse, oppression or anxiety.

Even when a marriage was a good one, the surviving spouse may feel relief because of new freedoms to pursue new interests and hobbies in a way that wasn't possible before.

> For a number of those who experienced "relationship relief," there was a sense of having paid their dues while the person was alive. Having been sufficiently threatened, humiliated, imprisoned, mistreated, and, in short, forced to give up so much, they feel nothing but relief now. What's more, they feel entitled to it.

This doesn't necessarily mean they don't have lingering problems with anger or regret or unfinished business of some kind, but it does mean that they aren't dealing with guilt.[3]

When working with people who struggle with guilt over their feelings, explore whether the guilt is tied into the feeling of relief or if it has been ingrained as a habit rather than a true emotion. Suggest establishing a guilt-free day each week, and on this day they practice becoming aware of what creates their guilt feelings, and then reject each one of them. This can be done verbally or in writing. It also helps to put up signs indicating that they are taking a vacation day from guilt, and that it's all right and even positive to enjoy a day without this emotional hassle.

Encourage them to evaluate which kind of day they prefer—guilt-filled or guilt-free. In time, they will move more toward guilt-free.

Barriers to Expressing Relief

A lack of social support increases the pressure to keep feelings of relief bottled up. "Who can I talk to about this?" Another pressure is to hear others say, "Oh, he was such a fine, kind man" when that wasn't the case at all. Having to put on a façade can lead to many conflicted feelings. One author said, "Unfortunately, we became the repositories of some deep, dark secrets. To be a relieved griever is to be a keeper of secrets—a lonely place."[4] Perhaps the fear is not only others' lack of understanding but their negative responses as well.

Another struggle in trying to move on with the relief is when there are painful memories because the deceased person was such a negative factor in their life.

Relieved grievers are so overwhelmed by conflict, anger and regret that they want nothing but to heave a huge sigh of relief, slam the door, and padlock it. But it's essential for future relationships that they come to terms with the wretched relationship. The past is always with us in obvious and subtle ways;

people with whom we have long-term relationships become, for better and worse, part of us.

Unfinished business can take many forms. Particularly if the relationship has been lengthy, survivors may define themselves according to the way the deceased saw them. They still see themselves in the role of victim, and satisfactory grieving involves nothing less than creating a new sense of self.[5]

Your task as a counselor will involve helping the person identify the pain and come to the place of relinquishing the events, some of which could involve trauma. The following questions and instructions, beginning with the subhead "Identifying and Relinquishing the Pain" up to the end of the chapter, just before the case study, are suggestions you can reproduce and use with the counselee. They are written in a format you can give to the griever when he or she is ready to face this issue.

Identifying and Relinquishing the Pain

To find healing today—and to set the stage for whatever the future holds—take a moment to think about your personal sense of loss with regard to this person. You have to face the past to confront the present. It's not easy. It can be painful. Many are reluctant to "face the unacceptable."

The *first step* is to identify what happened and when. Here are several questions that can help you do that:

- My relationship with _____ in preschool was . . .
- My best experience with _____ at that time was . . .
- My worst experience with _____ at that time was . . .
- My relationship with _____ in elementary school was . . .
- My best experience with _____ at that time was . . .
- My worst experience with _____ at that time was . . .
- My relationship with _____ during adolescence was . . .
- My best experience with _____ at that time was . . .
- My worst experience with _____ at that time was . . .

• My relationship with _____ during adulthood was . . .
• My best experience with _____ at this time was . . .
• My worst experience with _____ at this time was . . .

The *second step* in the healing process is to identify what is true about _____ and what isn't, what is factual, what has been reinterpreted and what you don't know about this person. Recovery could involve learning some things about _____ you would rather not know. As you enter this search-and-discovery phase of your journey, ask God to be your guide as well as informant. Ask Him to lead you to both the truth and the information you need to know.

How do you go about this? First, identify what you would like to know about this person. What questions you need answered. Then go to relatives and friends of _____ and simply ask your questions. Ask the person's co-workers, if they are available. Be aware that you will come up against contradictions as you go through this process. Perhaps the use of photos can help you in this process. Sometimes all it takes is a question.

The *third step* requires a trusted person with whom you can share. It's time to talk about your feelings about yourself, what you've learned and how you feel about what you learned. One of the best ways to begin is to *write down* how you feel (longhand rather than on a computer), because the "drainage process" that happens through physically writing your feelings can be very helpful. Sometimes it's best to talk first with a close friend, pastor or counselor, and then eventually a trusted family member. You may discover you're not alone in your thoughts and feelings.

The *fourth step* is important as well: Re-create the past. "Oh, if only it could have been different" is a comment I often hear. It's wistful thinking, but often followed with, "Oh well, no sense wasting time on that." But it's not a waste of time. It's helpful to dream about the way you think it should have been, because it helps you identify all the things you lost. No one else will do this for you, so you're the one to take this step and think about your past. You could do this in a number of ways. You could write the story the way you think it should have been or you could complete a series of "I wish . . ." statements.

- I wish my _____ had . . .
- I wish my _____ hadn't . . .
- I wish my _____ had said . . .
- I wish my _____ hadn't said . . .
- I wish my _____ would say to me today . . .
- I wish my _____ wouldn't say to me today . . .

Ball of Grief

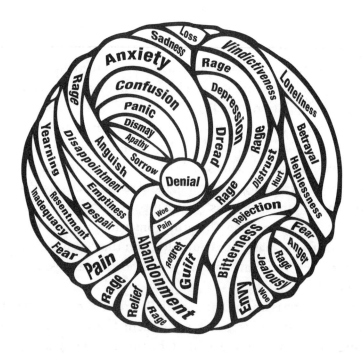

There can be a host of feelings underlying your losses. The best way to access your emotions is to look at your history and identify what you wish were true (which amounts to a loss), then look at the Ball of Grief illustration above and identify what you are feeling. If you're angry, write,

"I'm angry because . . ." If you're fearful, write, "I'm fearful because . . ." You need to express it in writing and then give it to God. Say to Him, "God, I'm giving You this. Take it and drain it from my life. I want to move on." Reading other books on loss, grief, anger, worry can give you some additional practical steps to take.

Another major step is choosing to forgive. The best definition of forgiveness is "wishing the other person well." It involves letting go. It is like holding a pen tightly in your hand and then opening your hand and watching the pen drop to the floor. Remember playing tug-of-war as a child? As long as the parties on each end of the rope were tugging, you had a "war." But when one side let go, the war was over. When you forgive _____, you are letting go of your end of the rope. No matter how hard the person may tug on the other end, if you have released your end, the war is over for you.

Imagine you're getting ready for a trip that you're really looking forward to. You bring out the soft-sided suitcase you just purchased because it can hold a lot. You begin to select the items you want to take with you. The piles seem to grow, but you should be able to fit everything in. Your suitcase begins to bulge and expand, but that's what it's supposed to do. Finally, you get everything in and sit on it so you can close the zipper. It doesn't have the same shape it used to, but that's all right. You try to lift it, but it barely bulges. The only way to get it to your car and the destination is to drag it. Already you're beginning to wonder if you need all this stuff, and if it's worth the hassle. The trip is beginning to feel like a burden rather than a pleasure.

This is the way it is for many who've been hurt. They wake up in the morning, fill a huge suitcase with all memories and hurts and then pack the real stuff—anger, injustice, resentment. Some have a mixture of feelings and memories—not only for what they missed out on but also for what they will never have. They also itemize how _____ _____ failed them and then add to it how they've failed themselves. It's just baggage, but it's excess baggage. And it's not like you can ship this suitcase on ahead of you. It's handcuffed to you, so you drag it everywhere—it weighs you down, drains your energy and hinders your progress. Worse yet, the suitcase contains things you don't even need.[6] You're carrying a grudge.

Forgiving may be difficult. But forgiveness is the one way to move ahead in life and experience God's abundance and grace. It's the ultimate step to healing a wound. You may not feel ready yet. You may not think _____ deserves forgiveness. But this is what forgiveness is all about. *None of us deserves forgiveness.* It's got to be a gift. It's a gift that will give you freedom.

One way to initiate your act of forgiveness is to write a statement of release. Here are some models that you can adapt for your own personal situation:

- I release you from determining how I respond to others in my life. I release you from the anger and resentment I have held toward you and others in my life because of you. This includes anger and resentment for . . .
- I no longer hold you responsible for my happiness. I release you from my expectations of who you should have been, what you should have done, and . . .
- I release you for not being there for me emotionally and for your silence over the years. I don't know why you weren't there. I don't need to know.
- I was mad at you for dying when I was a child and not giving me a chance to get to know you. I missed out on so much. I blamed you. I'm sorry. I hope you're in heaven.
- I forgive you.

Forgiveness, especially for years of neglect, abandonment or control, doesn't come easy. If you find yourself struggling to express positive feelings toward _____, you may have unresolved resentment hiding within you. There is a way to uncover those feelings and clear the way for moving ahead.

Take a blank sheet of paper and at the top write, "Dear _____ _____." Under the salutation, write the words "I forgive you for . . ."

Then complete the sentence by stating something _____ did that has bothered you all these years. For example, "I forgive you for not affirming me."

What is the first thought you had after writing your sentence? It may be a rebuttal to the forgiveness you're trying to express. It may be an emotional protest against what you've written.

Whatever your thought might be, write another "I forgive you for . . ." statement for it. Keep writing "I forgive you for . . ." statements for every thought that comes to the surface. Don't be discouraged if your angry protests contradict your desire to learn to forgive, or if they're so strong that it seems like you have not expressed any forgiveness at all. Remember, you're in the *process* of forgiving _____. Continue to write until all the pockets of resentment and resistance have drained away. Forgiveness won't occur until your anger toward the person is released.

Some people complete this exercise with only a few statements. Others have more resentment to clear away, and they continue writing for several pages. You will know you have completed your work when you write "I forgive you for . . ." and can't think of any more responses to complete the statement.

After you have finished writing, sit facing an empty chair and read your statements of forgiveness aloud. Imagine _____ _____ sitting there accepting your forgiveness with both verbal and nonverbal affirmation. Take as long as you need for this process, explaining and amplifying your statements as you go, if necessary.

Don't show this list to anyone; it's unnecessary. When you're finished verbalizing your statements, destroy the list. Burn it or tear it into little pieces symbolizing that "the old has gone, the new has come!" (2 Cor. 5:17).

The *final step* is to actually grieve. Grief is not an orderly process. It can be disrupted. The following steps have helped many people with their grief process.[7] [These steps can be duplicated and given to the person as homework or used in a session.]

1. Try to identify what doesn't make sense to you about the losses you experienced with the person. It could be the "why" question, which is both a question and a cry of protest. Even if the person could give you an answer, it probably wouldn't satisfy you. It's the same when we cry out "Why?" to God. If He ever answered us, we'd probably still argue with Him. You may wonder, *Did _____ ever love others? Did he have any idea, any guilt over what he didn't do for me? When _____ didn't come to my concert, did he know how much that hurt?*

2. Identify your emotions and feelings that you've already thought about or written down. Since this is an ongoing process, do you see any change in their intensity over a period of a few days? Is there an increase or decrease in these emotions? Remember, if you're facing some of the new losses for the first time, feelings can be more intense than before.

3. Identify the steps you will take to move ahead and overcome these losses you've suffered because of _____. It is a helpful way to identify what you've done in the past as well.

4. Don't try to handle your losses by yourself. Share this journey with someone else; and remember that your journey through grief will never be exactly like that of another person. Your journey will be unique.

5. If you know of others who have experienced a similar loss and recovery, talk with them. His or her story will have similarities and dissimilarities, but could be helpful.

6. Identify the positive characteristics and strengths of your life that have helped you in the past. Which of these will help you at this time of your life?

7. When you pray, don't hold back any feelings. Share everything you are experiencing with God.

8. Think about where you want to be in your relationship with _____ a year from now. Describe this in as much detail as possible. Put it into a story or letter to yourself, or express it as a prayer.

9. Understanding your grief intellectually isn't sufficient. It can't replace the emotional experiences of living through this difficult time. You need to be patient and allow your feelings to catch up with your mind. Expect fluctuations in your feelings and remind yourself that these fluctuations are normal.

10. One of the most important steps in recovery is being able to say goodbye. When you do this, you're acknowledging that you're no longer going to share your life with those hurts, unfulfilled dreams or expectations. For some people it's a one-time occurrence; others will need to do this on several occasions. One of the best ways of doing this is writing a goodbye letter and then reading it aloud as you commit the letter's contents to God.

When you're able to grieve, you are able to take care of unfinished issues in your life. Not addressing your losses keeps you cemented to the past. Saying goodbye is an important step in this process. Life is a series of hellos, goodbyes and hellos.

How do you feel when you say goodbye? Sad? Do you feel more a sense of "I wish it weren't so" or a sense of relief? The word "goodbye" originally meant *God be with you* or *Go with God*, and it was a recognition that God was a significant part of the passage. It helps to know that as you grieve you will be strengthened when you remember that God is there in your journey with you.

When you take the step of saying goodbye, eventually you'll say goodbye to your grief and hello to a new life.

Those who feel relief in their grief engage in what we call purging, or getting rid of reminders. This can include any type of items in the house, rearranging the physical space in the house or décor or getting rid of the house itself; a wheelchair or bed; sports equipment; phone messages; jewelry; and so on. Even though the death is, in some sense, a relief, it's not that easy, as one writer says:

> After a relief death, the future, which at first seems to unroll before us like a smoothly paved road, turns out to be full of potholes. What we envision as we sit at the bedside of a loved one can feel quite different after the bed is empty. We don't immediately comprehend the ways we have been changed.[8]

——————— C A S E   S T U D Y ———————

Pam

Pam: Norm, I came in because I've really been struggling with depression for the last couple of months. I feel like I made some mistakes when my loved one died. I just really knew he was getting sicker and sicker, and I felt like I should do something about it. At the time, I just kept thinking he needs rest and his body needs to recoup. If I had taken him in earlier, he might still be with me. I don't know quite how to get rid of the guilt I've been feeling. I keep blaming myself for his death.

Counselor: So, what I remember from your story, you said you waited about five or six hours and then called 911 for the ambulance.

Pam: Yes [nodding].

Counselor: Jim had been sick for a long time, you said about 15 years, with this cancer.

Pam: Yes.

Counselor: And it had gone elsewhere all through the body.

Pam: That was part of the struggle.

Counselor: But your sense is that you could have prevented his death.

Pam: At least at that time. He might have lasted longer if I had done something sooner to help him.

Counselor: Did you discuss this with the doctor?

Pam: I did, and he tried to reassure me there was nothing more I could do. For some reason, I keep thinking it is my fault. I'm having a hard time with that.

Counselor: If you could go back and recall that conversation with the doctor, what did he say?

Pam: He said that the cancer was widespread and it was eating away pretty much all of Jim's body at that time. It would have happened sooner or later. They couldn't really save his life long term because the cancer was so widespread.

Counselor: Did he say anything about Jim dying at this point— that there was nothing that they could have done either?

Pam: They said they could have probably put him on a machine. He would have been on life support. It would have prolonged the actual heart stopping.

Counselor: So you wouldn't have wanted him to be kept alive without really living.

Pam: Yes and no.

Counselor: A mixture.

Pam: Part of me would have wanted him still to be here, the other part of me realizes he was already gone and he would have been living without really being here.

Counselor: So there's sort of a conflict inside. What are some of the statements you make to yourself because of this?

Pam: Typically, I'm pretty harsh with myself. Like I should have called earlier; I should have seen that the symptoms were getting worse. I think it may be coupled with being a caretaker for so long.

Counselor: You were a caretaker for many, many years, weren't you?

Pam: [Nodding] Yes, that's why I'm so hard on myself. I was used to doing that.

Counselor: So there is a big loss there. There's nobody to take care of now. You're dealing with that as well. You know, I just wonder if Jim were here right now and we were to ask, "How was the care you received from Pam?" I wonder what he would say.

Pam: I don't know. He was a very gracious person; when I would do something for him, he always thanked me. He never took it for granted.

Counselor: He was appreciative.

Pam: He did appreciate it [agreeing].

Counselor: Could that have been because your care was really good?

Pam: Maybe. I think inside there were times when it was hard to do, and I sometimes resented it, but I tried never to show that.

Counselor: You pushed beyond the resentment to continue.

Pam: I felt that I needed to do that even though I didn't always want to be in that role.

Counselor: That's a really normal experience for a caretaker to go through. It's a blend of, "I want to help, but darn it, I wish we didn't have to be in this situation." That's for both him and for you. What I'm hearing, Pam, is that it's a little difficult for you to give yourself the benefit of the doubt. You tend to be a little hard on yourself. Maybe because you were a caregiver for so long, because you were in that role, maybe you could have stopped him from dying. It's a reflection on your ability as a caregiver, but in reality, you're a wonderful caregiver.

Pam: I guess I don't always have the power over life and death that I wish I had.

Counselor: We sure don't. No, we really don't. You know, guilt is normal. We all wish we could have done more even though we did everything possible. I'm wondering what would happen if you took some time and wrote out all the things you did for him so that you could see it.

Pam: [Nodding] I could do that. Yes, that's tangible.

Counselor: That is tangible. I think it will register more. You could also write out, "I don't have the power over life and death." You're looking at all the things you could have done, rather than what you have done. Would that be correct?

Pam: [Nodding in agreement] Yes.

Counselor: So you've tried that part of it and you've experienced the results, which is probably feeding your guilt. Perhaps if you swing to the other side of it you would probably see something different.

Pam: I think that would probably help. I could work on it. Just talking back to myself doesn't help.

Counselor: Well, I'm wondering what, if you did talk back to your guilt, you would say to it?

Pam: I would probably tell it that it's been here too long. That it's robbing me of joy and memories of the good times we did have.

Counselor: How would you like to say goodbye to guilt?

Pam: Probably write it a letter.

Counselor: Tell it to get lost because it's an unwelcome, uninvited tenant in your mind.

Pam: I know my husband wouldn't want me to feel guilty forever.

Counselor: You used the word "forever."

Pam: Yes, because it feels like I'll feel this way forever.

Counselor: I'm wondering if Jim would want you to feel guilty at all? I can imagine him standing here saying, "Thank you. You did a wonderful job. It's time for guilt to go." Can you envision that?

Pam: Yes, I think I could [nodding and choking up a bit].

Counselor: Why don't you give me a call next week and tell me what it's been like and where we can go from there.

Analysis

This case involved a multitude of emotions—guilt, depression, grief. To counter Pam's self-blame, it was important to look at the facts about her husband's cancer and what his doctor said. Pam lost not only her loved one, but her caretaking role and responsibility as well as her image of herself as a good caregiver. I tried to normalize some of her conflicting thoughts and feelings. There are times when it's helpful for the griever to actually talk back to himself/herself as well as to his or her feelings. If some of Pam's thinking processes were changed, some of her feelings would change as well.

Types of Death

Sudden and Anticipatory

Death comes in many forms, bringing with it varying degrees of pain, sorrow and grief. When it comes, it disrupts the life story of each mourner, but no one experiences the disruption in the same way. We cannot assume that we know how a person is experiencing grief until we hear the uniqueness of his or her story. Any and all preconceived ideas on our part must be abandoned until we discover his or her experiences and life circumstances. If I'm counseling a family in which a child has been killed, the grief of each sibling, parent and grandparent will be unique.

The author of the book *How We Grieve* talks about the unique vulnerabilities inherent in every person. Identifying these vulnerabilities and exploring them and their meaning is a way to help people become aware of what they are experiencing and assist them in moving forward. Grievers are vulnerable in several areas.

They are vulnerable in their connections with those who die. Objects, things, places, events and other people are always there to remind them of the loss. Personal items, where the person lived, as well as the places they frequented, their special days and events are all reminders as well as areas that impact those who grieve.

Grievers are also vulnerable to the loss of stability. Daily routines and life patterns have been disrupted. The more a griever was involved in the everyday life of the loved one, the greater the loss and adjustment. Grievers tend to see themselves as no longer a complete person now that their loved one is gone. It's difficult to go on with life "without," and many feel incomplete in their present life story. It's difficult to see the future as they once did, and many have said they feel "fragmented."

Questions to Ask

1. In what way do you feel there's a hole in your life at this time?
2. What are the most difficult "withouts" for you to handle at this time?

Many are vulnerable to the stress of unfinished business—plans and dreams for the future, conversations they meant to have or needed to have, not experiencing what they expected for the next five years, not being able to share yourself with them or not being able to say "Goodbye" or "I love you" or "Please forgive me" or "I forgive you." If the death was a child, the parents are denied the opportunity to nurture and teach and watch the child grow up.

Questions to Ask

1. In what way was there anything unfinished between you and your loved one?
2. What could you do about that now?
3. What do you wish you could have said to _____ (person's name) before he (she) died?
4. What do you wish he (she) would have said to you?

Some mourners are vulnerable to the continuing effects of a painful relationship. It's difficult to cope with loss when there were strong negative feelings complicating the grief. Some may experience guilt or anger over their feelings toward the person. Perhaps the grievers were ministered to or, just the opposite, traumatized by the deceased, or perhaps it was the other way around. Perhaps the person feels responsible for the death or for failing to meet the person's needs.

> Negative bonding with the deceased complicates a person's coming to terms with emotional grief, especially in its extreme form. They then long for the deceased differently. Their desire is not exclusively loving and affectionate; resentment, frustration and bitterness are likely to prevail and can bind them strongly. This kind of unfinished business challenges anyone profoundly. They struggle even to recognize and acknowledge the negative elements in the relationship with the deceased. Even when they do acknowledge them, they often cannot express or come to terms with them.[1]

Some may be vulnerable to "disenfranchised" grieving. The support of others at this time is vital, but for various reasons, others may not recognize or validate their grief. They may not see the loss as that significant and thus may not give the comfort and support needed or may make inappropriate comments. This can be devastating and can intensify the grief as well as feelings of abandonment and alienation.

Vulnerability can occur because of the circumstances surrounding the death. Sudden, unexpected and traumatic death can overwhelm as well as delay acceptance of the reality of what has occurred. Caregiving for months or years can exhaust and make it difficult to process grief.

Question to Ask

1. What was there about this death that didn't make sense to you or is difficult for you to handle?

Finally, many are vulnerable to limits in their coping ability. Even for those who have good coping abilities, they too may discover that what has worked for them before doesn't work at this time. The onslaught of intense and overwhelming emotions can create a paralysis. Weak areas that were well hidden before will emerge, and unresolved issues and losses from the past will resurface. Personal and relational dysfunctions may intensify. To add to all of these issues is the problem of our culture's inability to face death and the grieving process. Having to learn about the process of grief while experiencing its ravages is one of the most difficult tasks.

Question to Ask

1. What is the most difficult thing for you to handle at this time? What coping skills are working for you?

Perhaps these and other questions you create can assist you in understanding the uniqueness of each person's grief and assist you in helping them.[2]

Grief in Our Culture

Death in our culture is an avoidant activity, as is the mourning process. Some people respond in inappropriate ways for a multitude of reasons. Consider these descriptive words:

Grievers need ongoing support. Unfortunately, we try to provide the griever with a timetable that is not always appropriate for them. We imply that they should return to work within a week or so. We want to see the widow dating again, but not too soon. Our timetable fails to take into account the unique, individual nature of every relationship, loss and grief experience.

Much of our avoidance is rooted to our own fears associated with death and grief. We don't really know what to say to a griever. Our question, "How are you?" is asked in an attempt to evoke social conversation. We are not prepared to respond when the answer is, "I'm not doing well." Many of us would not ask how someone was doing if we thought they would give us an honest answer.

We also maintain a morbid curiosity about some deaths. If the death was a suicide or murder, we want the griever to tell us everything. This is not an attempt to help them in their grief, but simply voyeurism.

Then our attempts to provide comfort and support are often failures. We make statements such as *I know how you feel. They certainly lived a long life,* and *You were lucky to have them as long as you did*, which are meant to help, but rather show the speaker's lack of understanding. None of us can truly know how someone else feels in their grief. If we have experienced a very similar loss, we can have some understanding. But every death, every relationship and every person's grief is unique.

If we see someone we know grieving a personal loss outwardly, in public, we react very differently. Rather than validating their grief, we try to encourage *containment*. We avoid grievers who so outwardly show their emotions. We see this response as excessive and inappropriate. We try to get them to mute their grief. All too often the griever complies. He or she recognizes the discomfort of others. Accordingly, in public, the bereaved will not try to show the feelings and emotions that are inside. They learn to grieve in private over their own personal losses.[3]

A sudden death can make a shambles of schedules, priorities, agendas, and sometimes, our most intimate relationships. A loved one's last breath inevitably changes us. The experience can be paralyzing or it can be empowering. It can cause us to take life far more seriously.

Sudden death is more often heard than witnessed. Because of this, a person may feel anguish, wondering what the person's last moments were like, whether they were terrifying or painful. It is natural for their seconds or minutes of dying to become hours of emotional distress. Turning off thoughts by sheer willpower alone is not easy and often it is impossible.

The fact that they weren't there when the death occurred can also be a source of long-lasting regret. The fact that *no one* might have been there can also be stressful. They may have to deal with the painful mental process of second-guessing: *if only* _____ had consulted a doctor earlier, and so on. Sudden deaths are often bizarre, like nightmares, because they are so unexpected. This is especially true of accidents.[4]

To some extent, it is possible to experience survivor guilt after any death, even if the death wasn't part of some disaster. Why should we still be alive when someone else has died? *"If only* I had called the ambulance an hour earlier; *if only* I had persuaded _____ _____ to give up the job last year," goes through their mind. Surely there must have been something he or she could have done.

There are two key concepts that stand above others when it comes to sudden death. The first is *preventability,* which is not identified or addressed. But it has a major impact on their life. The person views the death as an event that didn't need to have happened. It wasn't inevitable. It could have been avoided. Often the mourner engages in what could be viewed as a crusade or a mission—to exhaust all efforts and resources searching for the cause, who's to blame and what should happen to them. They're searching for meaning in a senseless act, since their view of life and faith was violated. "Why? Why? Why?" is the cry. As one person said, "The unfairness and injustice in this longing for explanation boggles the mind, begs for explanation, and intensifies the emotions."[5]

The second issue is *randomness.* These acts are terrifying since there is no way to control them. Many mourners tend to blame themselves for what happened. It's easier to cope when you think it's your responsibility and, thus, in a sense under your control. Believing that "It was my fault" is a high price to pay for being under control.

Question to Ask

1. Is there a possibility that in some way you feel that you're to blame for this happening?[6]

Survivor guilt deals with the fact that people still consider themselves responsible and powerful in the face of death, even though all evidence proves otherwise. When one is used to making life better by his or her own efforts, it's hard to let go and admit there was absolutely nothing that could be done.

Linked to this is a certain uneasy feeling that his or her own need to live somehow contributed to the person's death. Here's what several have said about this:

"Until _____ got sick, I was eager to get married and have a baby. We had a wedding date all lined up, but she didn't live to see the wedding. I feel kind of superstitious about my plans, as if by planning my life I was being too selfish for them. My plans, my wanting to move ahead, took too much of her energy."

"When _____ was finishing with life, I seemed to be just starting my own. I had a need to live, and _____ had a need to die. Neither of us could change, but the contrast made me feel guilty."

The fact that a person's death removes the buffer between ourselves and death can also mean that guilt blends into fear. Thoughts of "it might be me next" or "it could have been me" are common.

Some people may have to come to terms with guilt over "not being good enough" as a child. The child's self-centeredness can be profound—that feeling that they're somehow responsible for everything.[7] With a sudden death, a person ends up feeling helpless and powerless. There's confusion over what happened and feelings of regret and guilt even months or years later.

When counseling, it's important to return objectively (as much as possible) to the event and consider several questions. In regard to _____'s death . . .[8]

- What was I able to do?
- What was I unable to do?
- What were others able to do?
- What made me feel that I was able to help?
- What made me feel powerless to help?
- Now I realize:
- What I miss most about _____ now is . . .

Even when a person carries memories of her relationship with the person, death carries a sting. It signifies an end to those intense years that have taken such a toll in life. The events themselves can never be forgotten, but the pain of the memories must be dealt with or they can keep a person snared by unhappiness.[9]

One of the most common issues in sudden death is no chance to say goodbye. Some goodbyes are verbal, while others are nonverbal. How did _____ say goodbye? Ask, "If _____ didn't say goodbye or was unable to, how might _____ have said it?" "Describe how you would have liked _____ to say goodbye to you and how you would have liked to say goodbye to _____."

Here is some information you could fill in during a session or have the griever complete at home and bring back:

- What I know about _____'s childhood
- What I know about _____'s adolescence
- _____ accomplished
- What _____ liked
- What _____ loved
- Those _____ was closest to
- _____ was happiest when . . .
- _____ was saddest when . . .
- What upset _____ the most
- Eight adjectives describing how _____ acted toward me

- What _____ was to me
- What I was to _____:
- _____ would like to be remembered for

A Different Type of Grief: Anticipatory

Anticipation can be a great part of life. For many, it's something that adds excitement to existence and an eagerness within. The word actually means "to feel or realize beforehand: foresee. To look forward to or to foresee and fulfill in advance." One of the most difficult times of life is when what we anticipate is the inevitability of someone's death. We tend to think of grief as after the fact rather than beforehand. Many of the people you will minister to will experience this type of grief. It can also mean "to act in advance, to prevent, forestall."

One wife said, "When all that remained was hope for my husband's survival, and he continued to decline, I felt absolutely helpless. My arsenal was depleted. There was nothing to do but surrender and redefine hope to be much greater than whether he lived or died. In the end, the effort 'to forestall' seemed to cause everyone involved suffering. At the same time, it was an integral part of the journey."

Trepidation—"trepidatory grief" would be a closer fit for the kind of grief people with a life-threatening illness and their loved ones go through up until the point where bad days outnumber the good ones.[10]

With a sudden death, a person's work is to deal with the aftermath and try to rebuild their life. In anticipatory grief, people have the opportunity to say and do things during the illness that may help them, help the dying loved one and the family members and friends. This could add to a more positive experience for everyone involved. If this is more of a positive experience beforehand, there will be a better bereavement experience after the death.

Anticipatory grief is not just focused upon a future loss. It's much more than that. As we work with those in this situation, it's important to be aware of the losses and help the mourner become aware of them. Remember this: The grief that a person experiences during the terminal illness of a loved one is actually stimulated by losses of the past, those that are occurring at the present time as well as those that are in the future. It's not unusual to remember what they used to experience and to grieve over all that has been taken away that they will never experience again.

Each day can bring new losses. If the person is slowly changing, is debilitated or losing control, there is grief over what is currently being lost and for the future that will never come. So anticipatory grief is both a mourning of what is occurring each day as well as what the future holds. A wife said, "The bad news is that all the grief done up front doesn't necessarily mean you get to bypass the grief after the death. The good news is that all the anticipating, which is not passively waiting for the big 'G' (grief) after the big 'D' (death), but actually grieving the many losses along the way, can help with adjustment and integrating the loved one's death. When it does happen, there's a well-worn path to the heart and grief isn't as likely to be the blunt blow it might be in a sudden loss."[11]

Sometimes family members begin pulling away from the dying person too soon and engage in premature detachment. They withdraw their emotional investment in the person prior to their death. Somewhere I read this statement that impacted my thinking and has stayed with me: "When we interact with a terminally ill person, are we responding to them as if they are dying or as if they are still living?" It's something to consider.

For anticipatory grief to be healthy, it's a process of starting to grieve now the loss of a loved one in the future without separating prematurely from them. Involvement is still important while recognizing what will occur in the future. As one person said, "It's possible to mourn the future without relinquishing the present."

As you sit and talk with those who are waiting for a family member to die, keep in mind that you're helping people in conflict think of what their loved one is going through. First of all, they're moving toward their loved one and directing love and energy and trying to make it better and easier for them. At the same time, despite their efforts to keep the relationship the same, they're also starting to move away from their loved one. It may be just the image they have of them in the future. It's like they're holding on to a person, letting go of them and also drawing closer.

Questions to Ask

1. What is going on in your mind as you watch what is occurring?
2. What's the most difficult part of this for you each day?
3. How could others be more supportive of you at this time?
4. How are some of the losses you've already experienced affecting your life?

Grief following the death is impacted the most by what occurs inside the griever. But with anticipatory grief, there are three factors impacting their grief: (1) what occurs within the person; (2) what occurs between the person and the dying loved one; and (3) what occurs between the person and the family and friends. Let's consider what may be going on within the grieving person as he or she awaits the death.

There are four sets of psychological processes, and they overlap. The first one is *a growing awareness and acceptance and a gradual accommodation* to the loved one's dying. Imagine that you are visiting a loved one in the hospital, and as time goes on you realize that the illness is much more serious than you thought, and the possibility of their not recovering begins to grow in your mind. At first you resist the thought, but soon you begin to come to terms with the possibility of that person's death. What occurs next is that you begin to rehearse the death and its impact and consequences. Then you begin to move into your role as an anticipatory griever.

Questions to Ask

1. When did you begin to grasp that _____ could be dying?
2. To what extent have you been rehearsing _____ _____'s death and what it will mean?
3. Can you describe for me some of the impact or consequences of _____'s dying?

The second set of psychological processes is *processing the death emotionally*. This is where a juggling act begins since you are dealing with a multitude of your own emotional reactions to the death while having to deal with demands of the other's terminal condition. This is the emotional process. As if this loss weren't enough, there will be mourning over past losses as well as present and future losses related to this illness. For many, at this point they begin to live more and more with fear and anxiety, and this creates even more pressure and stress.

They come to the place where the reality of the death is so real that they begin to withdraw emotional energy from the loved one as well as all future hopes and dreams. One day the realization hits that the loved one is going to die, while they are going to live. This can lead to considering how they can go on with their life "without."

Questions to Ask

1. How would you describe your emotional response at this time?
2. Which loss has been the most difficult for you?
3. When did you come to the realization that _____ _____ would die while you will go on living, and how did that affect you?

There are processes or thoughts that go on in the person's mind as they await the death. This is the third set that occurs. It can begin with an increased concern for the loved one. Thoughts seem to get stuck, and sometimes it seems as if they can't stop thinking about them. There's a gradual transition in the person's identity, roles, beliefs and expectations as they begin preparations for the new life without the loved one. They want to spend as much time as possible with them in order to remember as much as they can after they're gone. This includes sights, sounds, smells—all of the senses are involved. Many people conduct a historical review in order to capture the memories, for this is what is left after death. Some will bargain with God for more time or for healing. Naturally, there are thoughts about one's own death. One of the dilemmas some struggle with is how to handle the remaining time.

Questions to Ask

1. At a time like this, our mind often goes into overload with so many thoughts. What's been going through your mind?
2. What steps have you taken as you prepare for your life without _____?
3. What have you been saying to God at this time?
4. Often we think about our own death at a time like this—perhaps how and when, and do I want to die like this. What can you tell me about your mental journey?

This entire section has not been easy. Many thoughts and feelings were activated because I walked this path with my wife, Joyce, for over two years. I didn't realize how much anticipatory grief I was in until after she died. Part of my knowing that she would die from her brain tumors wasn't always conscious. The surgeries, chemo and radiation all held out the hope of healing, and our focus was on that; yet under the surface was the entertainment of another possibility—death. Perhaps that stemmed from the death of our son, Matthew, in 1990, after a two-week stay in the hospital for corrective surgery. The following is some of my personal journey after Joyce died, and it reveals the process I went through.

Unanswerable Questions

One of the greatest gifts we have ever received is our mind—our thoughts, and especially our imagination. With it we can be creative and resourceful and move forward in life. But it can also be one of the greatest sources of pain because of what we choose to dwell upon. What we think about and say to ourselves feeds our emotions and our grief. Imagination is to our emotions what illustrations are to a text or music to a ballad. Often we fixate on thoughts and questions that tend to plague the pathways of our mind.

I Wonder . . .

Do you ever wonder what goes through the minds of others? I have. I still do, and especially Joyce's, during her last weeks of life. And it causes me to wonder what I would think and feel were I in her circumstance and place in life. It causes me to wonder what I *will* think and feel when it is my time to die. At 70, and because Joyce is gone, that is much more real than ever before. I see it less as an ending and more as a transition, a beginning. The hundreds of cards and emails I have received in the past month have had the consistent theme that leads to a sense of comfort and reassurance. But every now and then I still wonder.

I wonder . . .

- What went through Joyce's mind each morning when she woke knowing there was a sleeping enemy within her head that could awaken at anytime . . . and eventually did.

- How much of her thoughts and feelings were for herself or for what this was doing to her loved ones. And knowing Joyce as I did, I think I know, since she cared so much for others.

- What she experienced when she asked, "How long?" and heard, "It could be two weeks or a month or two." What is it like when you are told the news and then experience the process slowly as symptoms intensify and the words and thoughts diminish? And what frustration it must have been to think you've said something clearly and then see the puzzlement and wonderment on the faces of others and realize you didn't say what you thought.

- Did the pain and discomfort at the last overshadow looking forward to going to heaven? Could she remember the comfort of the Scriptures? Could she remember and hear and feel our expressions of love? I hope so.

I have a number of other wondrous thoughts. But they will remain in this state, at least for now. "Finally, brothers, whatever is true, whatever is noble, whatever is right, whatever is pure, whatever is lovely, whatever is admirable—if anything is excellent or praiseworthy—think about such things" (Phil. 4:8).

Considering the Future

The fourth set in this process is *planning for the future*. It's difficult for some to think about the future without their loved one and what it will be like, but it's necessary to plan. This also involves considering the losses occurring now and what will occur in the future. There will be many decisions to make.

In planning for the future, there are three important steps. *A first step is giving your attention and energy to the dying person.* This means remaining involved in as many areas as possible and resisting the temptation to withdraw. There could be increased involvement as the end approaches in terms of energy, thinking, time, financial resources, and more. It's important to be flexible. The person who is caring for the other has to adjust to the person's deterioration and increased disability. They may have to engage in some painful tasks or see painful procedures and learn to handle those.

Some people handle it better than others. Ellen lost her husband in his early forties. What was important to her was keeping her relationship with him alive until the end.

She wanted to be sure that Michael knew he was loved, and that she had completed her relationship with him up until the moment of his death. Here is what she repeatedly told him: "I loved him, that I would always love him. I really didn't want to live my life without him, but I didn't get to make a choice about it. I would do my very best job to raise our children right. I was just glad that we got to spend the time that we did together. I thought it was a privilege to be able to have shared my life with him. I was grateful for the time that we had and to have had his children."

Ellen emphasized that the message of love had to be clear, leaving no doubts. I think if you're smart enough of a human being, you actually convey to the person that you love them while it has meaning and while it has emotion. . . . I think conversations that you have with people who you know are on borrowed time . . . even though we're all on borrowed time, we don't live like we're on borrowed time . . . I guess what I'm trying to say is that we should all live as if we all know we're terminal, because we all are terminal.[12]

A second step is resolving your personal relationship with the person. This can involve identifying and finishing unfinished business. There may be some awkward moments because of a difficult relationship. Or the dying relative was constantly critical, defensive, manipulative, angry. Sometimes it's difficult to overcome such issues, especially if they weren't admitted. It's also a time to share with the person, if possible, what he or she has meant to your life, as well as stating promises and planning the future with them. At some point in time, saying goodbye is completed.

Questions to Ask

1. Can you think of any unresolved business between the two of you or something that needs to be said by either party?
2. Mention that this may be a time to share with the person the 20 significant words, which are: "I was wrong"; "You were

right"; "I am sorry"; "I forgive you"; "Please forgive me"; "I love you" and "Thank you." Then ask, "Which of these would you like to express?"

3. How have you said goodbye or how would you like to say goodbye?

A third and final step is simply helping the dying person and responding to his or her last wishes. The mourners may help to facilitate the kind of death the person wants; provide support to express what he or she wants; join the person in viewing his or her life; talk with the person about his or her future life in heaven; assist him or her in any way that doesn't bring about other losses or a sense of embarrassment; discuss how the person wants to be remembered; discuss his or her preferences for the memorial service.

If there is time, the mourners may want to have a memorial service in advance so the dying person has an opportunity to hear the eulogies and perhaps give a blessing to family members.[13] This unique experience and ministry is now having a widespread acceptance. Here is a firsthand description of this event from John Coulombe, Pastor to Seniors at Evangelical Free Church in Fullerton, California:

We had been training our VIPs ministry team (Volunteers in Pastoral Service), who faithfully visited the sick and homebound, to record the testimony, history and life stories of these dear folk. I thought it would be good for our people to go through the exercise of recalling their past, especially when their present often was unpleasant, painful and lonely.

They were invigorated and energized as they told their stories, and when those tapes were played at their memorial services, we realized how powerful those moments really were and how deeply they reached down and touched the children and grandchildren who were gathered.

Then in 1995, Jim and Nancy Jeffrey walked into my office at church one day and Jim said, "John, I have prostate cancer and the doctors have told me I have days, weeks and months perhaps to live, but not a year. I've never died before—what would you suggest I do to get ready for that day?" I was stunned. I had not talked with anyone before who was so upfront about matters of death.

I quietly regrouped and responded as though I were asked this question often. "Well, Jim, let's begin with this question: Do you know where you're going once you leave this life? How's your relationship with Christ?" He looked at me and said, "Great . . . no problems or questions or concerns there. I'm sure of my faith and know where I'm going!"

I responded with "Okay, how about your relationship with Nancy? Is there anything that you need to make right with her that has been left undone?" Jim looked at Nancy and said, "Honey, can you think of anything I haven't made right with you?" She shook her head from side to side and said, "No, as far as I know, I think we're good." I then queried about the children and grandchildren. "Anything in your relationship with the kids that needs to be dealt with and resolved?" He and Nancy looked at each other and said, "I can't think of anything." The last question: "In your work as a real estate executive, were there any people you cheated or did wrong to that you need to make right?" His response: "I think I kept a good account on all those situations and made them right, John."

I sat there wondering what I was supposed to say next, and then these words came flying out of my mouth: "Well then, why don't we get together with all the family and have your funeral early so you can be there?" And then I got this look of wonderment from both Jim and Nancy, all the while hiding my own feelings of what I had just blurted out. They both looked at me and said, "What would that look like?" and I responded, "I really don't know, but I think it could be very meaningful and healing, as well as bring closure to your life as you wrap it up. You'll be able to say to the family and children what you won't be able to say to them when you're gone; and they will be able to bless and eulogize you as well, which they wouldn't be able to do when you're gone."

We agreed to meet together the day after Thanksgiving, which was when the whole family had planned to gather for their last Thanksgiving with Dad and Papa. And we agreed to bring in some video cameras so the moments would not be lost in time.

What a special time those three hours spent together were. We captured it on video. We returned two weeks later to record how the experience had impacted both Jim and Nancy, and to get feedback from the family.

Jim died two months later, and the following year we released a 14-minute video of the event entitled "We Love You, Jim," which CASA (Christian Association of Senior Adults) produced and released, which is still being used today to show the power words can have in a family when spoken as a blessing.

The word "eulogy" or "eulogia" means "to speak well of." We so often give eulogies to those who have died, when those words, if spoken sincerely, personally, face to face and heart to heart by those who carry each other's DNA, would have the power to heal, restore, renew and change one's course of life and thinking. So why don't we do it?

As I read of the blessings given by Abraham in the Old Testament, I don't recall God saying to us, "You don't need to do that anymore!" or "That was then and this is now, and is no longer necessary!" Abraham blessed his crops, his wives, his children and his God. The book of Psalms is replete with these words: "Bless the Lord, O my soul . . . !" God even wants us to speak well of Him; and I think He's still wanting us to obey His instructions, not only when we're in church or at home worshiping, but also in our homes with those whom we love the most on earth—our loved-ones.

You can't buy these blessings at Nordstroms. And if you could, you couldn't afford them. So why do we replace blessing our loved ones with expensive gifts from Nordstroms that, in the end, are "cheap replacements" for giving away ourselves, our affirmation and our blessing?

Perhaps it's because we feel guilty, uncomfortable, incapable or unable. Perhaps it's because giving blessings hasn't been a regular part of our lives, and our loved ones know us at our best and worst. My response is, "Get over it." It's not wrong to be where we are in this whole matter, but it's wrong to stay where we are. We begin where we are!

I think when we begin to formally find the words and feelings and speak or write them to our loved ones, we soon find those who are "blessed" responding favorably and with favor. But we must begin honorably by cleaning up any past "sins" or statements or actions that perhaps have been barriers with those family members and friends, so there are bridges for them to walk on back toward us.

Doing a "Living Eulogy" can become one of the most meaningful, life-changing events a family can experience together. Perhaps the living eulogy will become the newest sacrament of our age, bringing God's healing, hope, forgiveness, grace, wisdom and restoration to the Christian family . . . as well as to the unbeliever.

Ministering to the Dying

It's hard to imagine what it's like when you know you're dying. We can't understand those thoughts or feelings. A dying individual can be consumed by grief. We all know we're going to die. It's a fact. But when the word is given, it's still a shock. Then the losses begin. Think about them. Losses from the past, things done or not done, come back again. There are losses in the present because of limitations. Others treat them differently and talk with them differently because of the illness. They may sense the withdrawal of others. Then there are all the future losses, for there really is no earthly future anymore. For a believer, though, there is an unbelievably joyful future.

To minister to a person at this time, you need to understand their life and see it through their eyes. Can you list 10 or 15 of their losses and then imagine what those losses would do to a person?

Here are some possible losses: loss of control, independence, being productive, security, personal abilities (physical, psychological and cognitive), life experiences, future earthly existence, pleasure, plans, dreams, hopes, other loved ones, family's involvement, identity and meaning.[14]

Terminally ill individuals experience and struggle with many of the same feelings as the mourners.

Fears and Anxieties

With fear, the person knows what the threat is; but that's not always the case with anxiety. Let them do the talking. You can draw out what they are feeling with the following questions:

Questions to Ask

1. Of the fears you've mentioned, which is the most troubling?
2. When does the anxiety seem to be the strongest?
3. What have you done in the past to handle your fear and anxiety?
4. (If the person is a believer, there can be great comfort from reading Scripture and praying.) Ask, "What role does reading the Word and prayer play in helping you handle your fears and anxiety?"

A Variety of Fears

Many have said, "I'm not afraid of death, but I am afraid of the process of dying." Some of their questions can be answered, but some cannot.

There will be the fear of loneliness, the loss of family and friends and anything that has been left undone and unsaid. As a person's loved ones will mourn after he or she dies, the dying one will mourn their loss now.

If death will come from a progressive disease, there will be the fear of losing control of abilities and bodily functions. Many fear the loss of body parts as well. How will you handle the changes in body appearance when you see the person on an ongoing basis? They need people to continue to value and respect them.

Naturally, there is the fear of suffering and pain, and sorrow. One fear you may not have considered has to do with what happens at death—fear of mutilation, decomposition and even premature burial.

There will be numerous other emotions to respond to, such as depression, anger, guilt and shame. The presence of any of these emotions needs to be validated as normal and all right.

As you work with those who are dying, what is *your* greatest fear of ministering to a dying person? Of all the fears I've mentioned, which of those might you struggle with at this time? Our own concerns about dying need to be identified and confronted since they may be activated when we minister to those who are terminal.

Here's another scenario that allows you to walk in the shoes of the one to whom you are ministering. Imagine that you have been taken to the hospital and it was discovered that you are dying. You have a terminal illness. How would you like to hear about this? From the doctor? From your loved ones? This is what most would desire, but sometimes it doesn't work out that way. Now imagine that you hear the news in this fashion:

- You overhear one doctor telling another doctor or nurse.
- You overhear other healthcare staff talking about you.
- There's a change in the behavior of healthcare staff, or suddenly you are visited by those you haven't seen for a while.
- There's a change in medical care procedure, such as more medications, or surgeries that are postponed.
- Healthcare staff changes your location in the hospital or puts you elsewhere.
- Hospice personnel show up.
- You make your own self-diagnosis from the Internet, or by reading, talking with other patients or connecting the facts based on your own range of knowledge.
- Others avoid talking about the future with you.
- Even though some of these are indefinite, they raise doubts in your mind.[15]

Question to Ask

1. How were you informed of your diagnosis, and what was your response?

As in every counseling situation, allow them to tell their story even when they're dying.

In William Hoy's excellent book *Road to Emmaus, Pastoral Care with the Dying and Bereaved,* he offers the following helpful suggestions:

Good pastoral questions always indicate to the care recipient that we want to know more and are open to hearing as much of the story as he or she wants to tell.

I have often also used the question, "So, what are the doctors telling you about what is ahead?" followed by a question like, "And what does your gut tell you about that?" Seriously ill people do not always believe what doctors say. Even when doctors offer a chance of survival with a particular treatment, the critically ill sometimes suspect deeply that death is close, almost as if they have a "death intuition." In such conflicts, patients are the ones who are most often correct.

Everyone caring for the dying has heard of the dying person who refuses to talk about approaching death, and surely some of these people do exist. More often than not, an individual that does not want to discuss his dying with the pastoral caregiver is indicating a lack of confidence in the climate of the conversation or the willingness of the hearer to really listen. Dying people usually know deep inside they are dying and embrace the opportunity to discuss it—as long as they are confident their questions and concerns will be heard.[16]

When unsure of what a patient knows or believes about the course of his illness and whether or not death is close, try asking a somewhat vague but simple, open-ended question. A question such as, "So, John, what do you suppose is ahead for you?" may be met with a variety of responses, including, "Well, the doctors say I don't have long now" or "I'm not sure, I guess we're going to try this new round of chemotherapy."

Of course, some patients will respond with covert phrase like, "I guess I'm checking out pretty soon . . ." When this happens, be sure you ask a clarifying question like, "What do you mean 'checking out'?'" He may be using a euphemism for death or he might be referring to his discharge from the hospital![17]

Ministry to the dying requires patience. This seems ironic, considering that what the dying think they *don't* have is very much time. But time is required to contemplate the realities of life and death and to consider the overwhelming emotions and thoughts of facing death.

When engaging a dying person in discussion about the meaning of life, ask a question such as, "What is the best gift you have ever received? How about the best gift you have ever given someone else?"

The conversation might go in any number of directions. The dying person might offer a very deep, well-thought-out answer, perhaps indicating that he or she has been doing some thinking about accomplishments and heritage. If so, affirm the depth of the thinking and ask follow-up questions that invite more amplification to the story. My favorite is, "Really? Tell me more, would you?"

You know that death is "out on the table" by the phrases an individual uses. If a patient tells you, "It won't be long now," ask, "How long do you think?" and "What do you make of that?"[18]

Perhaps this chapter has raised issues or questions in your mind about your own death. If so, that's good. It's an area we tend to avoid. We know it will occur sometime, but why engage it in our mind before we need to?

Let me leave you with two questions to consider that we all need to face: (1) When do you think you might die? (2) After you die, where will you go and what will that be like? It's easy to give cliché answers or what we should say or what we want others to hear. But as we work with those who are dying, we will be brought face to face with our own mortality. What if the dying person asked you these questions? How would you answer?

8

When Grief Continues
Problems in Grieving and Recovery

There are occasions when recovery from a loss is disturbed for one reason or another. This is usually referred to as "unresolved grief." There are many reasons for this, some of which may overlap.

Unresolved Grief

In each case of delayed grief recovery, you will find some denial or repression and an attempt to hold on to whatever was lost.

Absent Grief

Absent grief is just what it sounds like. Feelings of grief and mourning over the loss cannot be found. It is as though the loss never occurred. Sometimes the person shows minimal signs of grief.

A minimizer is a person who is aware of his or her grief but works to minimize the feelings, diluting them through a variety of rationalizations. The person attempts to prove that he or she is not really impacted by the loss. Observers of minimizers may well hear them talk about how they are back to their normal routines.

On a conscious level, the minimizer may seem to be working and certainly conforming to society's message to quickly "get over" one's grief. Internally, however, the repressed feelings of grief continue to build and fester and, with no outlet, emotional strain and tension result.

This person often believes grief is something to be quickly *thought* through but not *felt*. This is typically an intellectual process in which words become a substitute for the expression of true feelings. Any feelings of grief are threatening to the minimizer, who seeks to avoid pain at all costs. It's true that some respond with thoughts first, but this person blocks all feelings.

Inhibited Grief

Inhibited grief involves the repression of some of the normal grief responses. The grieving person may be able to grieve only over certain aspects of what was lost. Perhaps he or she grieves for the positive aspects but not the negative ones. Other symptoms, such as somatic (related to the body) complaints, may take the place of normal grief response. Some of the more common somatic responses are stomachache, loss of energy or headaches.

A somatizer converts his or her feelings of grief into physical symptoms. This converted physical expression of grief can range from relatively benign minor complaints to the severely chronic pattern of multiple vague somatic symptoms with no physical basis.

Unfortunately, many grieving people unconsciously adopt this somatizer role, the "sick role," in an effort to get their real emotional needs—to be nurtured and comforted by the people around them—met. These persons often fear that if they were to express their true feelings of grief, others would pull away and leave them feeling abandoned.

Sometimes grief is delayed for an extended period of time, which could mean months or, in some cases, even years. It could be because of an overload of pressing responsibilities, or perhaps the grieving person feels he just can't deal with the grief at that time. When grief gets delayed, some other loss in the future may trigger its release and it may come like an avalanche. Even a very small future loss can be the catalyst to release the past grief.

A person who delays grief is called a postponer. He or she believes that if you delay the expression of grief, it will go away. Obviously, it does not. The grief builds within and typically comes out in a variety of ways that are not good for the mourner.

This individual may feel that if the grief doesn't vanish, at least at some point in time he or she will feel safer in experiencing the pain. Unaware that it is through expression that healing comes, he or she continues to postpone. The grief builds up inside the person, pushing toward the point of explosion, thus making him or her feel even less capable of experiencing feelings related to the loss. It is an unfortunate choice for handling grief.

Roy Fairchild's statement on delayed grief is very insightful:

> The refusal to mourn is the refusal to say goodbye to beloved persons, places, missed opportunities, vitality, or whatever has been "taken away," which is how many religious people view these losses. The refusal to mourn our earlier disappointments condemns us and rigidifies us, as it did Lot's wife. Genuine grief is the deep sadness and weeping that expresses the acceptance of our inability to do anything about our losses. It is a prelude to letting go, to relinquishment. It is dying that precedes resurrection. Our sadness reveals what we have been invested in; it is the cost of a commitment that has been shattered.[1]

Some people experience *conflicted* grief in which there can be an exaggeration of some of the characteristics of normal grief while other aspects that should be present are suppressed. Sometimes in grieving over a loved one, this reaction occurs because of having had either a dependent or ambivalent relationship with the person.

Grief Displacement

Another major problem response is displacing the grief. The displacer is the person who takes the expression of grief away from the actual loss and channels the feelings in other directions. For example, while not acknowledging feelings of grief, the person may complain of difficulty at work or in relationships with other people. Another example is the person who appears to be chronically agitated and upset at even the most minor events. While some awareness may be present, displacing usually occurs with no conscious awareness.

Some individuals who are displacers become bitter toward life in general. Others displace the bitter, unconscious expression of their grief inward and become full of self-hate, experiencing a crippling depression. At times, these people displace their grief in interactions with other people; at other times they believe people dislike them. Then, once again, they project unhappiness from within themselves to others.

The purpose of displacing is to shift grief away from its source and on to a less-threatening person, place or situation. Sometimes for the displacer, personal relationships become stressed and strained because the person is unable to acknowledge the occurrence of this common pattern of grief avoidance.

Chronic Grief

Chronic grief is a response in which a person continues to show grief responses that were appropriate in the early stages of grief. The mourning continues and doesn't proceed to any sign of closure. It appears that the person is keeping the loss alive with grief. This is especially prevalent in the loss of a person with whom the mourner had a very intense relationship with a great deal of emotional investment.

When a loss occurs within a family, it creates a major crisis. The family has been accustomed to functioning according to certain routines. Each person has his or her role, and this is critical to the organization and functioning of the family unit. A family unit gives protection and meaning to each member. Each person finds his or her own identity within the family and comes to understand that he or she is a separate individual.

When a family member is taken by death, there is an enormous vacuum within that family unit. The balance is disrupted. Not only are roles affected, but each person's identity is affected as well. A death forces each person to make some significant adjustments in his or her family role and the way he or she responds to the other family members. The giving of love, comfort and support may be a new role for some of the members, but the need for it is quite significant.

New roles have to be hammered out for each person; but before that can occur, they all need time and space to understand and handle the loss in their own way. One person might withdraw too much and become isolated unless brought back. Another may try to smother the others because of some of their fears. The new roles will have to be felt out until the family learns to function once again as a unit.[2]

Abbreviated Grief

Abbreviated grief is a normal grief response but can be mistaken for unresolved grief. There are several reasons for it: there could be an immediate replacement of what was lost; there wasn't that much attachment to what was lost; or, as happens in the case of a terminally ill person, much of the grieving occurs in advance of the death. Some people bypass the grieving with replacement.

A *replacer* is a person who takes the emotions that were invested in the relationship that ended in death and prematurely reinvests them in another relationship. For the most part, he or she is not conscious that the replacement efforts are really a means of avoiding facing and resolving grief.

Outsiders will sometimes assume that the replacer must not have loved the person who died if he or she can so quickly become involved in a new relationship. In actuality, often the replacer has loved very much and, out of the need to overcome the pain of confronting feelings related to the loss, avoids the pain by replacement. Replacement can include not only a person but also excesses in such areas as overwork or plunging frantically into one's hobbies.

There are three primary characteristics of unresolved grief: (1) absence of a normal grief reaction; (2) a reaction that lingers; (3) a distortion of a normal grief reaction.

When a person has one or more of these symptoms, and he or she continues beyond six months or a year, the person may have unresolved grief. The likelihood of unresolved grief increases as the number of symptoms increase. Some of these symptoms include a pattern of depression that lingers and often is accompanied by guilt and lowered self-esteem.

Depression and Mourning: Is There a Difference?

Depression is something we're all aware of, for it's a factor in so many lives. It's a common grief response; but what if a person had been struggling with depression prior to the death? How much is part of mourning, and how much is a carryover from before? What if you're dealing with complicated mourning and the depression that can develop from that situation?

It's important that grief and depression not be taken as one and the same. It's important that we become aware of the differences between mourning and depression. How can you distinguish between the depression of mourning and a depressive disorder? Here are some guidelines to consider.

Depression seems to have a life of its own. Its symptoms exist regardless of day-to-day events or triggers. The depression stays even in the absence of these events or triggers. Second, the signs of depression persist past two months' time, which indicates that the depression may not be occurring as a reaction to the loss.

There are a number of other factors that can clarify the differences.

A third factor: A person in grief is more likely to think, "Yes, this depression is normal for what I've been through, and it will lift." Someone who is already depressed is more likely to need help for his or her condition.

Fourth, grief doesn't bring the persistent, severe, distorted and negative perceptions of self and life in general that is characteristic of depression.

Fifth, the depression that comes with grief is usually the agitated, restless type; it tends to come and go and occurs earlier rather than later.

Sixth, guilt in grief is usually focused upon some specific aspect of the loss. Depression expresses an overall sense of guilt and is preoccupied with what the person has done wrong and how worthless he is.

In uncomplicated mourning, suicidal intent or signs are rare; but not so with clinical depression. With grief, there is usually a healthy mourning because the loss is acknowledged; but in depression, the person doesn't mourn.

With grief, pain is part of the loss and the mourner accepts it; but someone who is depressed doesn't see the value in pain. In grief there is a more overt expression of anger than in depression.

Grief is characterized by the experiencing and expression of a myriad of emotions, as well as variations in activity levels, communication, appetite, social functioning. This is not usually the case in depression.

In grief there is a preoccupation with the deceased; with depression it's preoccupation with the self.

Here are two final differences: (1) A person in grief often responds in a healthy and constructive way to warmth and support and encouragement; but someone who is depressed cannot; and (2) those in grief respond in a way in which others are prone to respond with sympathy and concern; a depressed person frequently will elicit irritation, frustration and a desire to avoid them.[3]

Here is a summary of symptoms that describe unresolved grief or delayed grief recovery:

1. A history of extended or prolonged grief that reflects an already existing difficulty with grief.
2. A wide variety of symptoms such as guilt, self-blame, panic attacks, feelings of choking, and fears.
3. Physical symptoms similar to those of the deceased person's terminal illness due to over-identification with the individual.
4. A restless searching for what was lost with a lot of purposeless, random behavior and moving about.
5. Recurring depression that is triggered on specific dates such as anniversary of the loss, birthday of the deceased person, holidays and even becoming the same age as the person who died. When these reactions are more extreme than normal responses, it can be indicative of unresolved grief.
6. Feelings that the loss occurred yesterday, even though months or years have passed.
7. Enshrinement or unwillingness to remove the belongings of a deceased person after a reasonable period of time.
8. Changes in personal relationships with other significant people following the death.
9. Withdrawal from normal religious activities and avoidance of usual mourning activities that are a part of the person's culture.
10. Inability to talk about the loss without breaking down, especially when it occurred over a year before.

11. Extensive thinking about and noticing themes of loss in life.
12. Minor losses that trigger major grief reactions.
13. Phobias about death or illness.
14. Excluding anything or anyone who used to be associated with a significant loss or deceased person.
15. A compulsion to imitate the deceased person due to over-identification with him or her.[4]

Linking Objects

Perhaps you've never heard about "linking objects," which can be partly responsible for a person's not moving forward to resolve the grief. A linking object is a symbolic object the person keeps that provides a means through which the relationship can be continued. Following a death, the grieving person may invest some object with symbolism that establishes it as a link between the mourner and the deceased. Sometimes it can be a piece of clothing or jewelry or a Bible. Some will wear or use the object for years and feel that it maintains a connection with the deceased. When a mourner has such an object, it's vital to them that they know where it is at all times. William Worden describes this:

> Linking objects are similar to transitional objects such as those that children hold on to as they grow away from their parents. As they grow older, they may hold on to a blanket, a stuffed animal, or some other object that makes them feel safe and secure during the transition between the safety and security associated with their parents, and their need to grow and detach from the family and become their own person. In most cases transitional objects are dropped as children grow up. However, when they are needed, their absence can cause a tremendous amount of anxiety and uproar.[5]

Sometimes items are kept to remind the person of good times together; but other times items are kept to remind the person of difficult times. Because these objects are so important, their loss generates anxiety. Most people keep something as a reminder when a loved one dies, but these objects have much more significance, and the grieving person can become very possessive and protective of it.

Ask the person what they have saved, what its significance is, how they would feel if it were lost, how it helps or hinders them in the grief process. Ask how long they think this object will be helpful to them. Some of these objects provide comfort and some provide connection.

Reasons for Unresolved Grief

Why do some people move through grief so well while others have such a struggle? Are there some common clues that can be identified? We have to allow for a variation of responses in grief, but for now we are considering recognizable unresolved grief. There are numerous factors that predispose a person to difficulty in resolving grief over a loss.

One reason for unresolved grief is that a person is unable to handle the emotional pain of grief, so he tends to resist the process. Another reason might be that the individual has an excessive need to maintain interaction with the person who is no longer there. This can be true for divorce as well as losing someone in death.

There are other reasons. Guilt can block grief. If we begin to reflect on our relationship with the person who is gone, we may experience excessive guilt over behaviors, feelings or even neglect that occurred in the relationship. If we have very high standards regarding our interpersonal relationships, it may not take too much to activate our guilt. This in turn blocks the grieving, since we feel unable to confront our guilt.

If you have ever heard someone say, "My life is a total loss without her. I feel like half a person. I cannot function without her," this could reflect an excessive dependence that in turn leads to an avoidance of grieving. This person tries to avoid the reality of the loss because part of the loss seems to be himself.

Some people resist grieving because the loss activates unresolved losses from the past that are even more painful for them to handle than the present one. Thus, an endless pattern of postponing the grieving is set into motion.

Overload may be another reason for unresolved grief. There are occasions in our lives when we experience a number of losses in a short period of time, and it is just too much to bear at one time. The losses are too heavy to face and handle. If a person loses several members of his family or even several friends at one time, not only does it produce overload, but he has also lost some of the people who could have given him support and comfort as he grieves.

Some individuals have never fully and adequately developed their individual identity. They haven't matured sufficiently, psychologically and emotionally, and whenever they are confronted with a loss, they tend to regress.

Still others fail to grieve because of a misbelief they hold on to. They fear losing control, for they have been taught that losing control isn't proper. They do not want to appear weak to others and to themselves. Some do not want to give up their personal pain because it ties them more closely to the person they lost.

The chart on the following page may assist you in identifying what is occurring with your counselee.

―――――― CASE STUDY ――――――

Trudy

Trudy: Right now, I'm on the verge of losing my job. I say losing it because I'm losing my ability to do my job. I'm feeling more and more overwhelmed. The biggest issue is I've been having some health problems lately and I can't focus. I keep thinking if I can't work, how am I going to support myself? So I didn't even realize how bad it was, and I don't know what to do right now.

Possible Warning Signs for Complicated Grieving

Avoidance of Grief
- Mummification (deceased's room is left unchanged long after the death)
- Idealization (exaggerating the positive qualities of the deceased, which maintains a fixation on the magnitude of the loss)
- Holding on to anger or guilt rather than saying goodbye and forgiving oneself and others

Chronic Grief (also called Prolonged or Interminable)
- Although the loss occurred years ago, the individual cannot speak of it without intense, overwhelming pain
- Years after the loss, unrelated events still trigger an intense grief response
- Themes of loss repeatedly come up in daily conversation
- Years after the death, the bereaved has not resumed normal day-to-day functioning

Delayed Grief
A current loss or other significant event that elicits an exaggerated response, indicating unresolved loss from the past exists

Inhibited Grief (also called Masked or Repressed)
- Neglect of health
- Drug abuse, including alcohol and medication
- Extended preoccupation with suicidal thoughts
- Acting out (promiscuity, legal violations)
- Persistent psychosomatic complaints, including chronic pain
- Developing physical symptoms of the deceased if he or she had been ill
- Impulsive decision-making (sudden radical changes in lifestyle)

Psychiatric Illness (may also be Masked Grief)
Psychiatric disorders (clinical depression, anxiety, brief psychosis, eating disorders, post-traumatic stress)[6]

Counselor: It's really hitting you now.

Trudy: It's really been hitting me hard. I realize I haven't been sleeping and I'm isolating myself. It just feels so stressful. I can't be there for other people.

Counselor: I hear tension. You also said you're isolating yourself; is that helping you with this?

Trudy: No, not really. I just feel like I don't even want to be around people when I don't have to be. I guess I'm trying to find a solution, and I'm trying to take care of things around the house, and everything is just overwhelming right now.

Counselor: I have something I would like to show you that might help to put this in perspective. I'm going to hand you a copy to take a look at [see the chart on the following page]. Let me explain this to you. What you've described to me really sounds like a crisis. You're probably familiar with that.

Trudy: Yes. [nodding as she looks at the chart]

Counselor: When any of us, you or I, or anyone else enters into a crisis, what we go through is somewhat predictable, and it helps us to know where we're at so we realize that we're somewhat normal but also see the likelihood of where we could go. If you look at that in the first phase, I don't know if this is what you experienced or not, because yours sounds like it's been more gradual. But sometimes people feel like they've been hit over the head with a mallet. They're sort of like, "Wow!" They're stunned and reeling. That's what it's talking about in the impact phase. You wonder, *What do I do?* You're numb and disoriented, can't function too well.

Trudy: Yes, I suddenly realized I hadn't done a bunch of things I thought I had done. There's so much I haven't done it makes me wonder where my mind has been, and then it makes me feel so inadequate.

Counselor: The second phase . . . you can see this could last from days to weeks, and it talks about the emotions being intense. They're going all over the place and they're bouncing around—

The Normal Crisis and Sudden Loss Pattern

Emotional Level

	Phase I Impact	Phase II Withdrawal/ Confusion	Phase III Adjustment	Phase IV Reconstruction/ Reconciliation
Time	A few hours to a few days	Days to weeks	Week to months	Months
Response	You question whether you should stay and face it or withdraw.	Intense emotions. You feel drained, anger, sadness, fear, anxiety, depression, rage, guilt.	Your positive thoughts begin returning along with all the emotions.	Your hope has returned and self-confidence begins to build.
Thoughts	Numb, disoriented. Your insight ability is limited. Feelings overwhelm you.	Thinking ability is limited. You experience uncertainty and ambiguity.	You are now able to problem-solve.	Your thinking is clearer.
Direction you take to regain control	You search for what you lost.	Bargaining and wishful thinking. Detachment.	You begin looking for something new to invest in or something significant.	Progress is evident. You form new attachments.
Searching Behavior	You often reminisce.	Puzzled, unclear.	You can now stay focused and you begin to learn from your experience.	You may want to stop and evaluate where you've been and where you're going.

anger, fear, worry, anxiety, rage; the thinking ability is limited, there is uncertainty, you're frustrated with the thoughts, *I can't put my hands on it, I forget things, things are ambiguous, they're not clear like they were before.* Sometimes with health issues, people start bargaining, "If I can get to the right doctor and he can do this for me" or "God, where are You in this?" Sometimes others say, "It's no big deal," but for you, I'm not hearing that. It sounds like to you it is a big deal.

Trudy: Yes, it really is.

Counselor: Yes, it's major for you.

Trudy: [Nods in agreement]

Counselor: It sounds like you're puzzled and unclear right now. Then as you notice the next part of the chart later on, many people in a crisis get to the place where their thinking balances out: "I can think of some positive things in the midst of all this crud that's going on." And they're not only able to think clearly, but they're also able to problem-solve. What's another alternative? "This is a health issue, what can I do?" Just from what I've mentioned here, where do you see yourself?

Trudy: I haven't been to the problem-solving stage. I'm not myself. I'm not at the problem-solving stage where I'd like to be. I'm seeing the result that I'm not okay.

Counselor: What would it take for you to get to that place?

Trudy: Probably admitting that I am concerned about myself. And not trying to do this by myself.

Counselor: On a scale of 0 to 10, with 10 being "I'm super concerned" and 0 nothing, where would you see yourself and your level of concern?

Trudy: Probably an 8.

Counselor: Pretty high then.

Trudy: That's quite high.

Counselor: It sounds like you've just admitted you are that concerned.

Trudy: Yes, I didn't even realize it.

Counselor: Who would you like to share that with?

Trudy: I have a close friend I could probably talk to about it, maybe more than one. Actually, just talking here is helping, not to be embarrassed about it. I'm used to doing everything . . .

Counselor: You're used to being self-sufficient, and you've moved into the other role of needing someone.

Trudy: That's a terrible place to be when you're a helper.

Counselor: That's a real bummer.

Trudy: It's a bummer. Actually, I should talk to my sons. [pausing] You don't want to bother your kids, but actually that's where I tend to isolate myself. I think, *I've got to take care of this,* and then come back and be around them. They probably would like to know.

Counselor: They probably would. They're no longer children or kids, they're adult kids, and they've moved to a different level where you interact sometimes as friends, and it sounds like they could be a pretty positive influence for you.

Trudy: Yes, they're wonderful. They're helpers too.

Counselor: So you have some built-in helpers.

Trudy: Yes, yes, I do.

Counselor: Do you see any others on this chart that you could identify with?

Trudy: [Taking time to look at the chart] You know, I think the "puzzled"; I was very puzzled because I kept thinking, *Why can't I do this?* I kept it in my head.

Counselor: And not reaching out.

Trudy: And not reaching out [with emphasis]. That's the hardest thing! I don't know why, I'm so used to telling everyone else to ask for help.

Counselor: You're so used to helping, but it's hard to reverse the role.

Trudy: I can solve my problems; I'm so independent.

Counselor: You notice the last phase, where it says, "Hope has returned."

163

Trudy: Yes.

Counselor: And "self-confidence has come back."

Trudy: It truly does when you remember what you have. There are resources that are very close to me that I love.

Counselor: In spite of the uncertainty, in spite of the unknown, there is the other side of it where we can eventually problem-solve; we can find solutions; we can reach out. And then maybe have a sense of hope. Is that a possibility?

Trudy: It's a big one now. You're not supposed to beat yourself up, but I could just kick myself for not reaching out. Just knowing that there are loved ones there means everything.

Analysis

This counselee has been a very functional professional person and has helped a multitude of others. At this time she is overwhelmed and struck with worry and negative self-talk impacting her emotionally as well as impacting her physical problems. Since she appeared to be in a crisis state, it seemed appropriate to use the Crisis Chart, so there was direct teaching involved in this session. The rest of the session was directed toward helping her identify where she was and take steps to begin to move forward. It's not uncommon for those of us in the helping profession to neglect reaching out when we need assistance.

9

How to Begin the Initial Session with a Grieving Person

Your initial session with a person in grief is foundational. Look at this person as if he or she is the only one in the world who has ever experienced such a loss and treat him or her accordingly. Early in grief we feel alone and believe no one could possibly understand what we are going through. Telling people that their grief is similar to someone else who has experienced a similar loss is not helpful. Our job or task is not to rescue people from their pit of despair but to hear their story and assess their situation.

A Model of Helping Others

One of the most helpful models I know for grief counseling is found in *The Phoenix Phenomenon* by Joanne T. Jozefowski. Keeping the following in mind can guide you as you minister to others.

Listen: "Tell me your story. I'd like to hear what you've been through" is a good beginning with each person. Hear their story with your ears, your eyes and also your heart. Hear it also with compassion, empathy and patience, for often there will be extended pauses as well as repetitions. If they say, "Have I already told you this?" a response of "Yes, but that's all right and I'd like to hear it again" will help. (For a review, see chapter 9 from *The Complete Guide to Crisis and Trauma Counseling*.)

Listen for emotions as well as body complaints. Listen for the times when their grief returns after moving forward. Listen for what they can't put into words.

Assess: Part of your involvement is to determine what the person's psychological, physical and behavioral needs are and how well they are meeting these needs and functioning.

Normalize: This is one of the most supportive steps you can take. This may need to occur verbally again and again but also by sharing with them the "Ball of Grief" (see chapter 5). They need your validation again and again that what they're experiencing is normal. It's vital to be realistic, positive and informative.

Reassure: Let the person know that he or she will be able to survive their grief journey although at times they may not believe this. You will need to lend them your faith and hope until theirs returns. You may need to remind them that support and help will be available. The phrase "You will get through this" is helpful. Remember, you can't give them a time or how their world will be a year or two from now. Let them know that you and countless others they're not even aware of will be praying for them as well.

Support: Help the griever discover or develop a supportive network of family, friends, neighbors and professionals. Help them to identify how they need and would like to be supported. Positive support reinforces their ability to express their feelings and concerns.

Plan: Planning is the heart of any type of counseling and coaching. This is a procedure that involves small, realistic and attainable steps. Plans need to be short-term initially. Everything decided on needs to be in writing so they can remember. Plans need to be adjusted and customized for each person. Co-design the plans with the grievers and encourage them to suggest the plans.

Clarify: Identify the griever's goals and purpose in the counseling sessions.

Intervene: There will be times when you may need to correct beliefs or even behaviors or plans. The way in which this is done should be gentle and supportive.

Educate: You will constantly be teaching in a direct or indirect manner. Printed material is necessary. Visual charts and graphs to plot progress will be beneficial at this time.

Monitor: Look for signs and symptoms of the griever being stuck, overly distressed or in serious depression, which may need additional assistance such as additional support, medical help, hospitalization, group support, and so on. As you learn these guidelines, they'll become a regular pattern to follow as you minister.[1]

What to Say

Here are some responses that I have made:

Sometimes those in grief come in and they don't want to be here to talk with me. That's understandable, since our being together can be painful. Many who come tell me they want to "resolve" what happened to them and get over the event and get "done" with their past. Unfortunately, there's no magic pill or therapy that can protect you from some of your memories or feelings or issues from coming back into your life. But by not facing it head-on, your present and future will be crippled to a certain degree. The more you fight facing it, the more energy you spend fighting yourself. Some actually try to pretend the event never happened. It doesn't work. Trying to do this is like trying to hold back a flood or trying to escape from quicksand. Now, since we both know this happened and it needs to be faced, what three steps can you take now to increase your efforts in moving forward and rebuilding your life?

It's important to remember what mourning or bereavement is and how we all move through it. This will help guide us in what we do and say. Chaplain Bill Hoy said, "Bereavement is a process of learning to fully experience the loss while still living with the memories."[2]

As you keep this framework in mind, it will help you determine where the person is in his or her grief and how he or she is moving forward.

Therese Rando has suggested a four-step process in ministering to a mourner that may help you. *Remembering* is the first step.

> Remembering realistically involves complete review of all recollections about the deceased and the mutual relationship. *All* means precisely what it says: the full range of memories of needs, feelings, thoughts, behavior and interaction patterns, hopes, wishes, fantasies, dreams, assumptions, expectations, and beliefs. It also means all of the aspects of each of these memories and all of the feelings about them—good and bad, happy and sad, fulfilling and unfulfilling, comfortable and uncomfortable, and so forth. The mourner must review completely all of what she knows and feels about the deceased and her experiences with him. This review—stretching back to the very beginning of the relationship—is necessary to put the mourner in touch with the entire range of memories and emotions that must be processed. Along with this must come a review of all of the meanings that various aspects of the deceased and the relationship, alone or in combination, held for the mourner. Whether views of the relationship are initially positive or negative, as the review process continues and if mourning is progressing in a healthy fashion, additional elements are incorporated.[3]

Recalling the significant and perhaps insignificant events and occasions helps in relearning the world without the person. We're back to having people tell their story in their own way and timing. Telling their story has two places. At first the telling is accompanied by pain. You can ask helpful questions to direct the person: What are the stories you can tell about _____ that bring a smile to your face? What are the stories and remembrances that bring the greatest pain? Who would you like to hear your stories about _____ _____ , and how could we make that happen? When do you find yourself longing for _____ the most? How do you handle that?

One of the goals, and something to encourage the griever with, is that someday the stories will be told without pain. That's the second place for the story.

A next step: *reaffirm* their values. It's a rare individual whose value system isn't either shaken or revisited by a death. It brings some closer to God and drives some further away for a while or permanently. Spiritual searching may occur immediately or after a time and is the same for a crisis of faith.

Questions to Ask

1. Can you describe how _____'s death has affected what you believe about life?
2. Has this experience drawn you away from or closer to God?
3. Since the death, how has your faith been impacted?

A third step: *Realize*. Others have different words for it, but it is accepting or realizing that a death has occurred. One of the most helpful steps in this process is seeing the body in the casket. We may hear about death, but we don't see it, and we try to avoid it. Death is a natural part of life. Even now, reading this, you may feel uncomfortable with this discussion. Death does not feel natural. Why? Because most deaths have been removed from our view unless we're in a particular profession. One fireman I worked with shared that he had handled more than a thousand bodies in the past 25 years.

Where have *you* seen death? Our great-grandparents probably died at home in their own beds with their family around them and while they were dying. Today, 80 percent die in a hospital cared for not by family but by paid professionals. There are few witnesses to death.

The last step: *Release*. It's another way of saying goodbye. It's a process of taking a step into our newly unfolding world. Releasing and saying goodbye may take awhile and may have to be repetitive. It's a process of "emotionally relocating the deceased," as William Worden said. William Hoy put it well when he said, "Bereavement is not a malady from which we recoil. To recover implies a return to the kind of life we previously knew, and such is not the case with those grieving a death loss."[4]

The following is an example of the first few minutes of a counseling session that incorporates some of the steps of the four-step process:

June: It's important that I start back 23 years ago and tell you what I've been through, since it reflects on my current situations. Maybe it will help you understand why I'm feeling the way I am and feel so isolated. Others don't really want to hear my story since they don't see how it relates to how I feel now and where I'm at.

Counselor: I'd like you to tell your story. This *will* help me understand more about you and who you are, as well as the present situation. Take your time, and if you need to stop at any time, just let me know.

June: I was married at 25 to what I thought was a godly man, and everything went well at first. A few years later, I discovered gay porn on our computer and confronted him, which he denied. We stayed together for several years, then one day I "discovered" him, and we divorced. At first I thought I had arrived with the man of my dreams, but those dreams died. I was single for three years and then remarried a quality man, or so I thought. Then the verbal abuse began. It continued. Three years ago, my first ex died, and I discovered it was from a sexual disease. Last year, I began losing energy. Now I can't work, and I'm waiting for test results. I don't know what's wrong. I fear the worst. I can't believe how much I miss my ex . . . I don't know . . . my life seems over.

Counselor: What you have shared with me says that many of your dreams have died. It's almost like a part of you has died, like you're experiencing the death of yourself while you're still living, and your ability to handle everything is not working . . . ?

June: It's true. I never thought about this as a type of death. I saw it as one loss upon another loss, another dream shattered. I've tried to handle everything; and the 23 years have not turned out the way I thought they would. I think of me then and then now, and it doesn't make sense.

Counselor: Perhaps you could think about this as a series of losses—of who you were in the past, and grieve over each one. I'd guess there are a number of these losses that you've never grieved over . . . is that a possibility?

June: It's more than a possibility. It's a fact. I haven't. I'm not sure where to begin.

Counselor: I wonder if it would help to begin by identifying each loss and then look at what hasn't died with you and use this to move ahead. What are your thoughts about that?

June: I guess we could. I appreciate any help at this time.

In this case, June needed someone to listen, to care, to clarify and to believe that she could move ahead.[5]

As you interact with a mourner, there are a number of specific questions to help you know more about the deceased as well as help the person recall what may be difficult to recall in the midst of their grief. These questions can help to activate recall of some of the purpose and meaning of the individual's life.

- What would you like to always remember about _____?
- What would _____ like you to remember about him/her?
- If _____ were here now, what would he (she) say to you?
- What was out of character for _____?
- What were _____'s favorite type of music and movies?
- What do you wish _____ had more of?
- What do you wish _____ had less of?
- What were some of _____'s qualities or strengths that you would like to have?
- What would you like others to remember about _____?

- How would you describe _____ to me?
- How would God describe _____?
- What would you like to say to _____ at this time?[6]

———————————— C A S E   S T U D Y ————————————

Diane

Counselor: Diane, you just called and made the appointment. I would like to hear what you've been experiencing at this time in your life.

Diane: My husband died, and he had done pretty much everything in the home all of our lives. I'm having to make decisions I didn't use to have to make. I have children who are acting up, in-laws who all of a sudden want to be in control of my decisions—wanting to make decisions that should be my decisions. I'm nervous about the consequences later on if I make a decision they don't like. My parents are calling about the grandkids. I am so overwhelmed I don't know what to do. I don't even know where to start.

Counselor: It sounds like you're torn in different directions.

Diane: Oh, yes, I'm torn. [nodding in agreement]

Counselor: How long were you and your husband married?

Diane: Twenty-nine years.

Counselor: What was his name?

Diane: His name was Tom.

Counselor: Tom. [short pause] Have you experienced many losses like this before? The death of a loved one?

Diane: No, not like this.

Counselor: It sounds like you have so many things going on in your life that it's difficult for you to grieve for yourself.

Diane: I don't even know where to start with my emotions. I don't know what to do or what to think. I don't know what should be more important, my kids or me.

Counselor: Could you tell me a little about what you're experiencing? Not with the children, your in-laws, your parents, but what's going on inside of you?

Diane: I feel lost and alone. I'm trying to figure out where God is right now. I believe in God, I'm just not sure where He is. I feel like He needs to give me an answer and tell me where to go right now so that I could know what to do. I feel lost right now. I don't even know how to do the simple things in life. When I get up I don't even know what to do, the first thing to do.

Counselor: Perhaps one of the first things is taking care of yourself and allowing yourself the opportunity to take time alone, away from others, and experience those emotions and just grieve. This is quite a loss for you, plus the added burden of some unfamiliar responsibilities and juggling everything. As you share with me your concern with your children, your in-laws and what they want, and then your parents, where would you like to begin?

Diane: Probably with my children. I'm sure they're very hurt and upset, probably mad at me. I just feel very sad to see them act this way. I know they're hurt, I know they're mad, but I just don't know what to do.

Counselor: Who are your children talking to about the loss of their dad?

Diane: When they're home, they're angry and not talking much. I'm really not sure who they are talking to or if they are.

Counselor: If they're not talking to anyone, and talking a lot to themselves, it just reinforces whatever feelings and distortions they might have. Do you have an opportunity to talk with them one on one?

Diane: I probably could. I could possibly do that.

Counselor: How would you do that?

Diane: They're all home at different times, and I could suggest that we sit down and have a talk. Ask if they would like to talk. And hopefully, they will feel they can and say their piece.

Counselor: Do you think it would help to take them to a restaurant where it is a neutral place, and not have the other kids come barging in?

Diane: [Nodding] Perhaps. We have a couple of places we like to go, and perhaps I could do that. I didn't think of that.

Counselor: Do you know how you would approach them to talk about this? [prompting her to go on]

Diane: I don't know. I don't know what I would say. I don't even know where I would start at this time, to be honest.

Counselor: Have the children seen you grieve in front of them?

Diane: Yes, they have. They've seen me cry; they've seen me be angry. They probably think, *Mom doesn't know what she's doing.* I'm emotional, so I don't know what I'm doing at this time.

Counselor: None of us know what we're doing in this stage of grief.

Diane: [Nodding in agreement]

Counselor: I'm wondering if it would help if you would be able to share some of your feelings. I'm going to be sending home with you "The Ball of Grief" that will help you describe what you're feeling. You can share this with your children, presenting it to them and asking, "Where are you in this?"

Diane: That would be helpful to me. I feel like I don't have a lot of words to start this conversation. This would be very helpful to start.

Counselor: I think the material that you'll take with you will give you some of the structure you're looking for. Your children probably feel abandoned because Tom—your husband, their dad—died. This way, if you get them alone, say, "I want to be with you." It might even help for you to say, "As we talk, I might lose it, and that's okay for me to cry, and I'll get it together and we can move on; and if you cry, that's okay too."

Diane: [Nodding]

Counselor: I'd like to switch to the in-laws for a moment. Diane, it sounded like you're feeling some pressure from Tom's folks.

Diane: Yes. [nodding]

Counselor: What has been their role in your marriage with them over the last 29 years?

Diane: They're nice people. They do offer opinions sometimes when they're not asked.

Counselor: Like most do.

Diane: I don't know how to . . . I feel like the decisions I make are decisions for me to make, not for them. I feel a little upset that they're coming down so hard on me. They're not just suggesting, they're demanding. They've always been demanding in subtle ways over the years. Very subtle ways. We just kind of ignored it when Tom was around; he took care of it; but he's not here now. Now I have to take care of this.

Counselor: It sort of sounds like they've moved from being subtle to a little bit direct.

Diane: I think it's because Tom's not here.

Counselor: Yes, and they're used to him being the buffer; and now they're thinking maybe we can influence Diane. What would you like to say to them?

Diane: I would like to let them know how much I loved their son. I want to definitely make the right decisions. I would also like to ask them to respect my wishes at this time since he's my husband. I can make the best decision; or I will make the right decision for Tom, but I'm afraid to say that to them. I'm afraid they won't really understand that I really do make the right decisions. I wish they would trust me with this, but they don't.

Counselor: So what would be the best way to convey this to them?

175

Diane: I don't know. I guess telling them?

Counselor: If you tell them, what is your fear about their response?

Diane: They're so demanding. I don't feel like I can be honest with them. I'm afraid there would be unkind things said about me, [pausing] and that it might get back to my children. I'm not sure. I am afraid of things they might say, just because they seem so demanding.

Counselor: If you were to engage them in conversation, they might not really hear you, and they might come back and continue to push you and talk you into it.

Diane: Yes, that's my concern.

Counselor: So, what is a better way to convey this?

Diane: Maybe I could write something. I like writing, and I use journals a lot. I always have. Do you think that's something I could do?

Counselor: A lot of people do that because it takes away the instant reaction, where they can think about it; they have to consider your perspective. It might be safer for you.

Diane: Yes, I would feel safer.

Counselor: Would you like to bounce the letter off of me before you send it?

Diane: Yes. [enthusiastically]

Counselor: I would be glad to help.

Diane: That would be great.

Counselor: It's important to think about everything you'd like to convey to them, affirming them in their concern and also telling them, "Here's what I'm planning to do . . ." What if they don't fully accept what you've written?

Diane: Another letter? [laughing]

Counselor: Well, that could be; or when they engage you in conversation, maybe all you have to do is repeat what you said in the letter without deviating from it. There's an old technique called the "broken record" technique, for those of us who remember records, when they got stuck. You can say, "I appreciate your concern, however, this is what I'm planning to do." And when they come back again, you can say, "I appreciate your concern, however, this is what I'm planning to do." You just repeat it two or three times, and as long as you stick to your script, you'll be in control.

Diane: That sounds good. I think I can do that. [hopeful]

Counselor: Also remember that as you're working through this, everything you do could trigger off these emotions. And everything will take longer than you expect. How will you handle your own folks? It sounds like they want you to come back home to live.

Diane: They have always wanted that. I kind of figured that would happen, so I'm not surprised. It doesn't bother me like my in-laws do. I feel like I can talk to them and they'll listen. I'm not surprised by their reaction. I think I can deal with them with conversations on the phone, and they'll respect me; they always have, and they've always been there for us, but not involved like the in-laws have to be. So I don't have fears with my folks.

Counselor: One of my concerns is that you are dealing with this loss of Tom, after 29 years. And then you have to juggle your children, the in-laws, your parents . . . do you have someone in your life who is a close friend that will walk through this with you?

Diane: I have a couple of very close friends I think will be willing to walk with me through this. We've been close for a long time. They have already been calling, and they're involved. They seem to be calling so that I'll know they're there. I feel like I can call them anytime. I feel comfortable at the church I go to.

Counselor: So there may be some people there?

Diane: Yes.

Counselor: Who are the people you don't want to help?

Diane: My in-laws. [laughing quietly] I don't have fears of anybody else. I'm not worried about anyone else right now.
Counselor: Thank you for your willingness to talk.

Analysis

This case is quite typical of a grieving spouse who feels overwhelmed by
life and who is attempting to meet the needs of everyone else but her.
Reflecting back her main feeling, rather than responding to each problem, lets her know that I hear and understand her struggle. It's important to guide the conversation to her grief rather than the people
problems. Even though she is not sure what to do, the questions are
structured to help her take the responsibility for the solutions. I went
back and forth, from questions to giving some definite suggestions on
what she might do. Some of the statements were for the purpose of
teaching her about the grieving process.

10

The Family in Grief

It's usually not one person impacted by the pending death but an entire family unit. Unique problems arise. The balance of the family system is disrupted, usually starting at the time of the diagnosis or before. Each member of the family unit differs in his or her response and even acceptance of the news. Some members will respond well to the needs of the dying person, while others would rather not acknowledge the impending death.

Each family member's grief is unique. You will become aware of this quickly, and the fact will stretch you and your ability to assist them. No matter whether you meet with a family of three or four or a group of eight or ten, each one will respond in a unique way, even though they have all been exposed to the same loss. But have they really? Perhaps, but perhaps not. It could be that you've already experienced this in some of your own grief events. Each person's grief response is affected by numerous factors, and by its own DNA. It helps to look at a mourner and realize all that has come into play.

From the Mourner's Point of View

First of all, consider the uniqueness of each loss. For each mourner, find out the following:

- What is the significant meaning of this loss?
- What were the qualities of the relationship with the deceased, as well as the security of the attachment? (Very close, close, distant?)

- What were the roles performed by the mourner, which have now been lost?
- What were the positive and negative characteristics of the deceased?
- What are all the secondary losses?

Before continuing to read, look again at these characteristics. Whenever you work with a mourner, have this grid of items in your mind or even on a small card; if the mourner doesn't talk about them, you may want to bring them up. Look at each one and formulate the questions or statement you would use to explore each issue.

Second, it's important to know something about the mourner. You need to see him or her as a unique individual. Think about these questions: (If the individual is struggling with his or her grief, it might be difficult to determine immediately some of these characteristics.)

- What is the person's personality? How does he/she usually cope and what has he/she done before? What are the indications of the level of the person's mental health? Is there a previous pattern of anxiety, depression, or . . . ?
- What is his/her belief system, faith, meaning of life?
- How would you describe the person's level of maturity?
- What are the other major losses the person has experienced in life, and when?
- What does the person believe or understand about grief and mourning?
- What is his/her cultural, social and faith background?
- In addition to this loss, what other life crises may the person be experiencing?
- What type of support network does he/she have?
- What is the level of support available from the network?
- Does the person have a description of the death? Was it experienced firsthand or by a notification? Was the death expected or was it sudden? Was there any indication of it being traumatic? What questions does the person have about this death? Was there

anticipatory grief? How does the person describe his/her grief at this time, as well as the grief of other family members?
• What type of service was there? Or will there be one that will require the person's involvement? Is there any present or future legal involvement?

Finally, look at the person's physical responses. Is there any use of drugs, prescribed medication, coffee, alcohol? What about the impact on eating habits, exercise, sleep and physical health?[1]

When a family member dies, the family balance or family unit dies as well. There's a hole in the fabric of the family, and not everyone will realize this. If something affects one family member, it affects the others. The family is a system, and it needs the support of each member to keep functioning. A family will need to identify all the roles that the dying member fulfilled and reassign them, which is easier said than done. In most cases, the older the person the more roles may need to be filled. Unless the roles are fulfilled in some way, the family will stay out of balance.

One metaphor portrays the family as a machine with various parts that need to work together to maintain its working order:

In certain respects, one may imagine the family as a complicated machine consisting of a series of complex, interlocking gears, which correspond to individual family members. Some gears are small, others large; some seem to serve a more important function than others, some seem less vital. When properly assembled, the machine operates beautifully, each gear interlocking with its companion in elegant precision. The machine purrs along, accomplishing whatever it was designed to do. Periodically the gears may need oil, and on occasion they may need some minor maintenance as a result of the normal wear and tear to which machines are prone. But a break in a single tooth, in even a minor gear, may have a crippling effect on all the other gears, and the machine may completely lose its ability to function and grind to a halt. The machine will remain inoperative until all the damaged gears have been repaired, and then it will not operate at high efficiency unless the entire mechanism is rebuilt and recalibrated. The machine has no ability to compensate for a malfunction in its component parts; it either works or it doesn't. This is the fallacy in the mechanistic metaphor; families, unlike machines, do not entirely cease operation when one member breaks down. Rather, they continue to function, albeit in a different way, and one mechanism that makes this possible is homeostasis.[2]

Some of the unique problems to consider in a family system are:

1. How close was each family member to the dying person? What was the quality of the relationship or the level of attachment?
2. What is the grieving pattern of each person and what does each know about grief?
3. To what extent does each person want to be involved with the dying person at this time?
4. How does the expression of grief affect the grief of other family members?
5. How will the family handle "after death" issues if there are differences, such as what type of funeral, disposal of remains, type of service, disposal and disbursement of clothing and personal effects, photographs shown or not shown, holidays, anniversaries, and so on?
6. What are the specific reasons for the grief of each family member?

When counseling, you need to look at the deceased and his or her position in the family and what the loss is. To a spouse, this will be the death of a spouse and all of its ramifications. To a child, it's the death of a parent. To a parent, it's the death of an adult child. It could also be the death of a sibling or in-law, or grandparent or favorite aunt or uncle.

Some had daily contact while some had much more intermittent contact. Educating each family member about grief and sorting out the grief myths may be a task, especially if there are younger children.

The loss of one of its members throws a family into crisis. To understand the enormous stress a mortal blow inflicts on the family as a whole—and on each of its members as well—it is helpful to consider the family's functioning methods during more routine times. The healthy, unstressed family operates under certain systems. Each member in the system is related, by both heredity and emotion, to each of the other members, and each member is crucial to the family's organization and balanced functioning powers. The family unit provides protection and sustenance to its members and gives a sense of belonging and togetherness. Each member finds his own identity within this unit and realizes that he is a separate individual.

A death disrupts the delicate balance between the family togetherness and its members' individuality. The deceased held a specific role of importance to the family structure. Eventually, the remaining family members will assume these responsibilities, the surviving parent taking on those obligations that require an adult's experience and the children filling in with those abilities that are in keeping with their ages and development. Until this occurs, though, the positions are altered, and the family's normal patterns of transaction are short-circuited. Before new and successful family patterns can be established, each family member must make significant adjustments, changing not only his role as a family member but his relationship to every other family member as well. This is not a step easily taken in the midst of suffering.

Before the construction of new roles can begin, each person needs time and space to absorb the loss in his own way. All members must maintain the ability to disengage, when necessary, from the unit. But disengagement can be carried too far.

Confronted with grief, family members are caught between the pull of sympathy for another's loss and the egotistical needs of their own bereavement.

Shortly after his mother's death, nine-year-old Jeff, pained by his father's need for seclusion shouted, "You've lost your wife, but you can get another. I can never get another mother!"

While the family suffers a collective loss, it must not be forgotten that each individual of that family now stands at the center of his or her own private tragedy.[3]

There are two major family tasks that tend to help the family move forward immediately and long-term in a healthy way. The first is *shared acknowledgment of the reality of death and shared experience.* It's like saying the family that grieves together moves on. Every family member, no matter what age, and in their own way, must confront the reality of a death in the family. This includes the children.

Nancy Bowen, a noted family therapist said:

I urge family members to visit dying family members whenever possible and find some way to include children if the situation permits. I have seen a child hurt by exposure to death. They are "hurt" only by the anxiety of survivors. Well-intentioned attempts to protect children or "vulnerable" members from the potential upset of attending such events isolates them from the shared experience and risks impeding their grief process.[4]

My own granddaughter attended three of her grandparents' funerals by the time she was five. Including all the members of a family means that death and what it means is talked about openly, and grave sites are visited. Family communication is a must over the course of the terminal illness and after, as is tolerance for the diversity of grief expression. It's also important that each member of the family have the freedom to express any feelings. The authors of *Living Beyond Loss—Death in the Family* said:

When feelings are unbearable or unacceptable, they may be delegated and expressed in a piecemeal fashion by different members. One member may express all the anger for the family while another is in touch with only sadness; one shows only relief, another is numb. When a family is unable to tolerate feelings, a member who expresses the unspeakable may be scapegoated or extruded. In addition, the shock and pain of a traumatic loss can shatter family cohesion, leaving members isolated and unsupported in their grief, risking dysfunctional consequences.[5]

The second family task is *reorganization of the family system and reinvestment in other relationships and life pursuits.* We discussed this earlier. There are two tasks within this that need to be carried out—*realignment* and *redistribution.* In order to recover, the family needs to realize and identify the relationships and redistribute the roles.

When counseling, think about how you will approach these tasks as you work with a family. Here are some suggestions:

- I would like each of you to think of two or three words to describe who you are during this time of waiting, as _____ _____ approaches death. (family)
- I'd like each of you to describe the grief you're experiencing. (family)
- Who in the family do you think is struggling with his (or her) grief? (individual)
- Let's talk about the roles and tasks that _____ fulfilled in the family. How are these roles being redistributed? Are there any roles that will go unfulfilled? (family and individual)
- What roles or what changes in the way your family used to respond would you like to change? (family or individual)

We've talked about the fact that each family member plays a significant role in the family. There is a family balance. When a person enters the family or leaves it, the family is off balance. The more influence or significance the deceased had the more imbalance will occur. Try to determine the significance, as it will help you identify the potential adjustments. It may not always be the parents' roles; think about the various roles family members play and what happens when they disappear.

The *doer* is the one who provides the maintenance functions of the family. The *enabler* provides the family's emotional and relational nature and a sense of belonging. The *loner* is the one who's in the family but more or less forgotten. The *hero* is the pleaser who brings recognition to the family through his or her success and achievement. *Mascots* are the family clowns who lighten up the family atmosphere. *Critics* are the family's faultfinding negativists. The *scapegoat* is the family victim. *Saints* express the family's spirituality.

As you look at the various roles, it becomes apparent why some family members may not feel loving toward one another. One case I worked with included an adolescent son who was the hero, the mascot and the saint and was very enmeshed with one of his parents. The other children were what I called background children. The grieving continued for years.

A second fact to consider is the emotional closeness level of the family. The closer the family may mean the more intense the grief.

Since emotional expression or venting is so important, you will need to assess this level. Do the family members have permission to express and not express feelings? Are they encouraged or hindered? The more that feeling expression is encouraged the healthier the atmosphere. If not, grief can be hindered. Functional families move forward.

William Worden describes the family structure and response in this way:

> The way in which a family construes the loss of a family member greatly influences how they grieve. A family that understands the death of a family member as a long-awaited relief from pain is likely to grieve differently from the family who construes a death as something that should have been prevented (Nadeau, 1998, 2001). Research has shown that families who

cope the best after the death of a family member are more cohesive; are more able to tolerate individual differences among family members; have more open communication, including more open emotional sharing; find more support from within the family as well as outside the family; and cope more actively with problems.[6]

As you work with the family, reach out to the children. They tend to be the forgotten grievers. (For additional information, it would be helpful for you to read the three chapters on children in grief and crisis in my book *The Complete Guide to Crisis and Trauma Counseling*.)

Here are a few additional guidelines on helping the child in the family when a parent dies. Research indicates that children who do well tend to come from a more functional home where communication about the deceased was easy and the home was relatively stable. The more stress there is in the family, and a surviving parent who was not responding well, the children did not do well. Actually, the greatest predictor of how a child would do was the functioning level of the remaining parent. The loss of a mother is harder on a child than the father. If children attend or participate in the funeral, they need preparation in advance.

Many children continue to connect with the deceased parent in many ways. They talk to them, feel watched by them, think about them, dream about them and actually locate them somewhere. Children need the following:

- They need support, nurturance and continuity.
- They need to know they'll be cared for.
- They need to know the death was not caused by anything they did or didn't do.
- They need detailed information about the death in a way that's appropriate for their age.
- They need to feel involved, important, have a continued routine and someone to listen to their questions.
- They need numerous ways to remember the person.[7]

Guidelines to Remember

1. When a parent dies, the entire family experiences a period of upheaval as the comfortable pattern of transaction between its members is disrupted.
2. In order to establish new, successful patterns of transaction, each individual in the family must adjust his own role and relationship to every other member.
3. Recognize that during the beginning weeks of grief the individual needs of family members may disrupt the family's ability to function successfully as a unit.
4. Individual griefs progress to different levels at different times. Family members must look beyond the walls of personal loss if understanding within the family is to be achieved.
5. Remember that each member of a family that has experienced a death sees himself at the center of that loss. Each individual lives through his own private tragedy.
6. Recognize the need for a good balance between family togetherness and individual freedoms. Encourage this.
7. The family needs to learn to respond to family members' needs without suffocating the needy individual.
8. Too much dependence between family members can destroy the boundaries that protect individual growth.
9. Allow each individual the scope to absorb the loss in his own way and time.
10. Suggest they do not let the walls between individuals grow insurmountably high. Don't respect privacy at the cost of the necessary sharing of grief.
11. Realize that children (particularly the eldest child) may feel compelled to try to assume the role of the lost parent.
12. Parents need to protect children from taking on inappropriate responsibility.
13. If the death was a parent, the one remaining can hasten the redevelopment of family cohesiveness by accepting their role

as the family's leader and the responsibilities that once belonged to the other.

14. If there is a sole surviving parent, they need to discuss decisions with knowledgeable friends instead of placing inappropriate responsibility on family members.

15. Recognize that as children grow from one state of maturation to another, family relationships and boundaries must be redefined accordingly.[8]

Questions about the family and the responses of its individual members are the most powerful tool for gaining a new understanding of a family. Are dates of death barely remembered, or honored as holy rites? How comfortable are family members in talking about the deceased and the circumstances of the death? Are both positive and negative memories available? The more information family members have, the more perspective they will gain on themselves and their lives, and the better chance they will have to face the future with openness.

There are also questions we can ask about loss in the family in order to understand the adaptation of previous generations that sets the stage for current family relationships:

1. How did various family members show their reactions to the death? Tears? Withdrawal? Depression? Frantic activity? Did they talk to each other about the loss?

2. Who was there at the moment of death? Who was not present who "should" have been? Who saw the dead body and who didn't?

3. What was the state of family relationships at the time of death? Were there unresolved issues with the person who died?

4. Who arranged the funeral? Who attended? Who didn't? Who gave the eulogy?

5. Was the body cremated or buried? If cremated, what happened to the ashes? Is there a tombstone?

6. Did conflicts or cutoffs occur around the time of death?

7. Was there a will? Who received what legacy? Were there rifts over the will?

8. Who goes to the grave and how often? Who mentions the dead and how often? What happened to the belongings of the dead person?

9. Was there any secrecy regarding the cause or circumstances of the death? Were facts kept from anyone inside or outside the family?

10. What mystification or mythology has been created in the family regarding the dead person since the death? Has he/she been made into a saint?

11. What difference do they think there would have been if the dead person had survived longer? What dreams were cut short by the death?

12. Do family members feel stigmatized by the death? (e.g., a suicide, a death from AIDS)

13. How have the survivors' lives been influenced by their relationships with the dead person? What do they carry with them from this person?

14. What are their cultural and religious beliefs about afterlife, and how have their beliefs influenced their understanding of the meaning of their loss?

15. What other beliefs do family members have that may help sustain them in the face of loss, e.g., a sense of family or cultural mission, a sense of survivorship?[9]

It will be up to you to decide when and how these questions are asked.

Here are some steps to help a family adjust to life "without" the person who has died.

First, one specific intervention is to have each family member write about what life was like with the deceased person and how life has now changed with this person's death. You might invite each one to draw a large circle on a piece of paper. Then have them divide the pie to illustrate the various roles they occupied prior to the death of his or her loved one (including the role with the deceased and all its manifestations). The size of each piece should correspond to the percentage of importance and the amount of time allocated to that role played in his or her life. Once they have completed the assignment, use the pie chart to discuss more fully the many facets of the role he or she fulfilled in the deceased's life before the death in contrast to how those roles may have changed subsequent to the loved one's death. Encourage them to explore how that empty piece of the pie might be filled as more is learned about how he or she is without the loved one.

Another helpful exercise is to ask each family member to write a list of both interests and activities they have pursued within approximately the last 10 years, indicating as well their level of interest in those activities as compared with the person who died. This may help the bereaved family to develop a clearer sense of their own personal interests dependent of the influence of the deceased person. Grief work is a journey to discover who the bereaved person is now as an individual subsequent to the loved one's death.

A third helpful activity is to have an adult person draw a genogram of the existing extended family to examine the nature of their current relationships and what their expectations might be for those relationships in the future. Death obviously changes dynamics in relationships—some of the changes are painful, but other relationships may grow closer and more meaningful. The bereaved person may also become aware of the need for additional friendships or more diversity in relationships. Suggest to them the use of a series of concentric circles to illustrate the nature and intensity of current relationships.

With his or her name on the innermost circle (the bull's-eye), invite them to add the names of people who would be the next most intimate in the second circle, the third most intimate in the third circle, and so on. They can put more than one name in each circle and can omit circles altogether if he/she decides that no one fits that category. This exercise provides a visual representation of the number and type of relationships of the people who are potentially available to care for and support him or her in the bereavement process. The exercise can also help the client to visualize how he or she might wish to adjust relationships within the concentric circles as his or her life takes on a new shape.[10]

A Summary of How to Help the Family

The following are additional suggestions as you work with family members, individually or corporately. If you were a medical doctor, your patient would not be an individual; it would be the family. It's the same for us as well.

First, you need to get to know this family as well as the culture of the family. If they are a different cultural background than you, talk to others to learn some of the distinctions of this culture. A friend of mine asks the family he's working with, "What do I need to know about your culture that will help me help you at this time?"

Listen to each of the family members to find out what they know, imagine, feel and fear. Don't assume that they understand all of your terms. Ask them questions to clarify what they know.

Remember that a family is a system, and it's important to meet together. I do this when I'm conducting a debriefing in companies and organizations when they've lost a long-term employee to death. We talk about the fact that this group of 10 to 20 individuals in the debriefing was his "work family," and they've just lost a family member. Those in the group concur, and it's vital that I meet with the entire group and they listen to one another, as well as to what I have to say. At work, it's just a larger system.

As you work with family members about the death of their loved one, ask about the person's work. Have the family indentify those people they are aware of at work. There are probably fellow workers who are impacted as much or more than the person's own family. You may want to contact the deceased's place of employment to offer your services at this time.

As you work with the family, attempt to build a relationship with each one. The more verbal ones will try to dominate your involvement. Remember that the quiet ones have as much to say as those who are outwardly verbal. They're talking to themselves. It's easy to neglect those who are quiet, as well as children. If you haven't worked much with children, it would be helpful to expand your knowledge at this time. (See footnote 11 for resource suggestions.)[11]

Discuss their fears and concerns about death as well as being around someone who is dying. Involve everyone in the care and treatment of the dying person. There may also be some individuals, relatives or friends that the family would rather not have as visitors. Identify who these people are and offer some practical advice on how to keep them away. Prepare to encounter some surprises and unexpected intruders.

Help the family find a way to express and download their feelings after every visit. Perhaps they can talk or pray or write out what they're experiencing for five minutes before they get in their car. Each person needs his or her own individual minor debriefing or the pressure will begin to pile up. Caregiving can be draining. Help them anticipate how this experience will stretch their own coping skills and be exhausting. Help them develop a plan for maintaining energy. Parents who are losing their spouse and still have to care for their children are especially vulnerable. Teach them how to handle one day at a time. Hopefully, your church will have some trained caregivers who can assist at this time.

If you are working with more than one family unit, be sure to activate your flexibility and adapt your responses and what you say and do for each family and person. What do you know about death and dying? What have you seen and experienced? Note that one of your tasks may be to educate the various family members, from children to adults, about death and dying. This can include what is anticipatory grief as well as what a dying person experiences. You may need to explain to the family what can be expected at the time of death or afterwards. They may also need assistance in finding resource materials, and financial and social assistance. Discuss their support network; and if there isn't any network, assist them in creating one.

Talk with them about those things they are hesitant to talk about. Some may feel guilty about planning the future without the person, or how this is affecting finances and the pressure of "who gets what" after

the person is gone. If you see this issue, you can say, "Often families struggle in talking about certain topics such as _____
_____. I wonder if this has been the case for any of you."

Help the family members to know how to respond to the dying person. Encourage them to let the loved one know what he or she has meant to them and how this person will be remembered.

Help them retain some level of optimism. "It's true that _____
_____ is dying, but how can you make the most of the time you have left together?"

One of the difficult times is when it appears the death is about to occur and, on his or her own, the person rallies and recovers, and then this pattern occurs several times. This can put the family on an emotional roller coaster.

Family members may wonder if their responses are normal since they may detach as a means of protection of their own loss. On the other hand, they may feel abandoned because the dying person will withdraw and detach since that is part of the dying process.

Help the family mourn together in a supportive way. What has been discussed in other sections of this book on death and grief will come into use here.[12]

One last suggestion has to do with you, the reader, and your own personal debriefing. You may be impacted by what you hear and see, so it's important for you to express and download your own feelings and grief that you experience in helping others. Talk with a trusted friend, write out your experiences, and pray. Remember that you, too, need others in your life in order to effectively minister to others.

11

Helping Grievers Move On in Life

Recovering

Everyone who grieves wants to move on. Some struggle with believing they will ever be able to do that. But the disorientation of grief will diminish. How will they know that their disorientation is coming to an end? There are several signs to indicate they are adjusting and recovering. Here are some main signs.

One of the first signs is *a sense of release*. It's a turnabout in the focus of their thinking. Instead of thoughts being locked to the memories of a loved one or wondering what they would be thinking or doing, it's more of thinking about living one's own life now and for the future. A person will reach out more and feel as though he or she is living life. As one woman said, "My sorrow now feels less of an oppressive weight, more of a treasured possession. I can take it out and ponder it, then put it safely and carefully away."

Another indication is *the renewal of their energy*. The fatigue begins to lift. They can renew activities that they wanted to engage in before.

A third change is *the ability to make better judgments*. It usually takes longer for this to occur than most would expect. Decision-making involves concentration, and those in grief find this difficult. Thoughts are jumbled, and staying focused is a challenge.

Finally, a person will *start eating and sleeping better.* How long does it take to see these signs of recovery? For many adults it seems to take 18 to 24 months before these four indicators are present. But many factors come into play to affect the amount of time recovery takes.[1]

Many ask for a specific road map for their recovery. *What do I do? How will I know that I'm getting there?* Here are some guidelines that show they have navigated toward healing and recovery:

- They will be able to handle the finality of the death.
- They will be able to review pleasant as well as unpleasant memories.
- They will choose to spend time alone and enjoy it.
- They can go somewhere without crying most of the time.
- They begin to look forward to holidays.
- They are able to help others in a similar situation.
- They're able to listen to their loved one's favorite music without pain.
- They can sit through a worship service without crying.
- They can laugh at a joke.
- Their eating, sleeping and exercise patterns are returning to what they were before the death.
- They can concentrate on reading or watching TV.
- They will no longer be tired.
- They can find something to be thankful for.
- They begin to build new relationships.
- They begin to experience life again.
- They will be patient with themselves when experiencing a "grief spasm."
- They will begin to discover new personal growth from grief.[2]

Recovery—moving on—involves many significant physical elements. Diet is one. It may be difficult to eat at this time. Food has lost its taste but not its nutrients. A person in grief will need a substantial and balanced diet. It doesn't need to have taste right now. Throat and stomach may resist, but encourage the person to override these feelings.

Exercise is another important element. It can reduce stress and anger. The grieving person may need to write a note as a reminder to make a commitment with a friend to engage in exercise at least three or four times a week.

Rest and sleep may be a struggle, but because grief drains energy, one needs more of both. The person may need to discuss this with a physician if sleeplessness is an ongoing problem.

Perhaps this picture of recovery resembles what your counselee is experiencing:

Recovery from loss is like having to get off the main highway every so many miles because the main route is under construction. The road signs reroute you through little towns you hadn't expected to visit and over bumpy roads you hadn't wanted to bounce around on. You are basically traveling in the appropriate direction. On the map, however, the course you are following has the look of shark's teeth instead of a straight line. Although you are gradually getting there, you sometimes doubt that you will ever meet up with the finished highway. There is a finished highway in your future. You won't know when or where, but it is there. You will discover a greater sense of resilience when you know in advance what you will experience and that you're normal in your response.[3]

And so, as they continue remembering, the pain will subside. Now the pain may be shouting, but someday it will whisper. The ache in their heart will go away. They may not think this is possible at this point in their life, but hearing these words about the future can make the present more bearable. If the person is a Christian, grief is different. It's infused with hope. The foundation for this hope is found in the death and resurrection of Jesus Christ. "He is the Lord over every loss and every heartache. He is the Lord of all comfort and mercy. He is the Lord of resurrection, restoration and regeneration. He is the Lord of life."[4]

You can direct the counselee to the hope that will return to replace the despair. The dust of drought and the dark clouds will diminish. One day there will be a smile instead of a frown, a calmness instead of being on edge. When? When they've gone through their grief and fulfilled their time. Knowing how long doesn't make it easier. "There is a time for everything, and a season for every activity under heaven . . . a time to weep and a time to laugh, a time to mourn and a time to dance" (Eccles. 3:1,4). "The LORD will be your everlasting light, and your days of sorrow will end" (Isa. 60:20).[5]

Helping those in grief is about establishing a relationship. Building a connection with them is foundational to helping them. Hearing their story, normalizing their feelings, educating them about the process and reflecting what you're hearing and sensing from them are the core of the process. There are many other steps or suggestions you can apply as you walk alongside the one who grieves. These will be based out of the framework of your believing in their ability to grow as well as your fulfilling the role of being an encourager. There is a biblical pattern for encouraging (see chapter 12 on the subject of grief coaching).

In this chapter, there are numerous suggestions to challenge you to think creatively of ways to help those in grief. You will need to determine when to use the various approaches described.

First Step: Getting the Big Picture

A first step that can be very beneficial is to complete a loss history to group the effect of the losses the person has experienced. The example on the following page gives you the framework to use. You may want to complete a history for yourself prior to using it with counselees.

Many grievers find that conducting a "life review" is an important step in accepting the loss and building a new relationship with the one *who has died*. The life review should include all aspects of the relationship, both the positive and negative. This retrospection helps grievers move forward as they revisit their memories and learn to selectively recall and treasure those that bring comfort and strength. They join memories of what they had with the sorrow for what they have lost.

A Loss History

Loss	Age	Experiences (feelings/behaviors)	Unanswered	What changed?
Death of Spouse	55	Felt my life ended	Why? How? What will happen to me now?	Felt my life was over—no one left, too young for this
Cancer	48	Fear of it returning; fear of dying; desire to not think about it	Will the chemo work?	My future; my lifestyle; my appearance
Diagnosis	47	Good support from friends	How long do I have?	My security; tremendous anxiety
Daughter had miscarriage and then hysterectomy	45	Devastated—Fear of never having grand-children	Why her? Why me? Where is my future?	My future as a grandparent was stolen
Son killed in war	43	My life was destroyed; anger at President; I was afraid of this anger	God, why? Why the unfairness?	My life, my hopes, my confidence in God
Lost two jobs in one year	37	Felt like a victim	Why me? Why not those flakes?	Security
Death of Parents	35	I miss them. Elderly, so not surprised	Not much	——
Home burglarized	30	Felt violated—unsafe; had to move—became hyper-vigilant	Why in this neighborhood?	Security, trust, overly cautious

The recollection of positive memories is especially important in helping tragic death images to fade, particularly if a violent death has occurred. "People often recall the bad times rather than the good times they had with someone they loved. That can make the yearning less, but it also keeps them distant from the positive feelings they had with the lost person. This prevents them from being able to resolve the loss."[6]

Beginning to Let Go

A person in grief can also move forward in the letting-go process by writing a "Letting Go" letter. This generates feelings, but it releases them as well. It moves them along the recovery process and brings healing. Some read their letter out loud by themselves or to a trusted friend. The content of the letter could contain details about one of the most special times they ever experienced with their lost loved one; what they miss, what they wish, what they wish they could still talk about; what has been most difficult during the time of grief; what they will do to remember the one who has died; and what has been learned through this loss. These subjects may bring up others to write about. Have the counselee conclude the letter by stating that he or she is in the process of letting go and experiencing life again. Remember, this is an honest expression. Here is a sample letter:

Dear . . .

This is a strange letter. I never planned to write to you after your death. But your leaving has left a painful hole in my life. I don't like the empty grieving feeling I have inside. I miss you. I miss it all—your voice, your presence, your laughter, your raising eyebrows, your stubbornness. You know what else I miss? Your dreaming out loud. I miss our dreams and the future we won't have here together. I feel cheated. This was not the time for you to die. Or it wasn't the time I thought you should.

I've cried buckets of tears over you. I've cried for me and raged at you and God and me and everyone else who still has someone. I've wanted you to come to me, and I wish I could come to you. I don't like being alone. Oh, I know there are others around, but they aren't you!

It's been months. I've stabilized now. I'm learning to rest in the hope that someday, some way we will see each other. I'm taking a big step now. I am taking baby steps to go on with my life. I feel strange saying this to you, but you went away, you were taken from me, but I have been holding on to you. Now I'm letting go to live life again. I have our history together, memories together, and a rich life because of you. Thank you. I'm letting you go, but I will not leave you. I will have to let you go many more times. I know that, I miss you. I love you. You are not forgotten.[7]

Perhaps they've been in their grief for a while. There are two questions that will need to be addressed at some time or another. They are different, even strange: (1) *Has the person committed himself/herself to a certain amount of time to grieve?* Some do that unintentionally, and some do it intentionally. One may have heard that it takes two years to grieve if it is a natural death, three for accidental death. Don't let any of these suggested time frames dictate recovery time. Don't set a time frame unless it's all the time that was needed. Keep it open-ended. (2) *Has the person given himself/herself permission to stop grieving at a given point in time in the future?* Think about it. People in grief will need to give themselves permission to *stop* grieving. Throughout grief they will say goodbye to the one they lost, and eventually say goodbye to grief.[8] Remember, life is a series of hellos, goodbyes and hellos.

Most goodbyes carry a sense of sadness, a feeling of "I wish it wasn't so." Do we ever look forward to goodbyes or get used to saying the words? Probably not. Many goodbyes lead to heartache. The word "goodbye," originally "God be with you" or "Go with God," was a recognition that God was a significant part of the going. Perhaps we have forgotten that along with the journey we gain strength when we remember that the Giver of life is there to protect and console, especially when the goodbye is because of death.[9]

A goodbye creates an empty place, which causes a person to ask questions that need to be asked: *Why suffering? What do I believe? How will this goodbye impact my life? How will I be different?*

We all need to learn to say goodbye, acknowledge the pain that is there for us so we can eventually move on to another hello. When we learn to say goodbye we truly learn how to say to ourselves and to others: God be with you. I entrust you to God. The God of strength, courage, comfort, hope, love is with you. The God who promises to wipe away all tears will hold you close and will fill your emptiness. Let go and be free to move on. Do not keep yourself from another step in your homeward journey. May the blessing of our God be with you.[10]

If the deceased loved one knew Jesus, and the person grieving knows Jesus as Savior, goodbye is just for a season. One day they'll say hello again. Their loved one is just going to the banquet table before them. Just imagine the loved one in the presence of Jesus, experiencing the joy of His closeness!

Saying goodbye is one of the significant tasks of grieving. It begins with accepting the reality of loss, working through the pain, adjusting to life without the loved one, withdrawing emotional energy from this person and reinvesting it elsewhere, and, finally, changing the relationship with the loved one from one of presence to one of memory. Saying goodbye is part of the concluding process.[11]

The Healing Benefit of Letter Writing
Letter writing can be a key step in helping mourners work through their grief. Some may feel uncomfortable with the process, but your encouragement can help them break through their resistance to this healing step.

Begin by having the person write a letter to his or her Grieving or Devastated Self. It could be a specific part or aspect of the person's life. Perhaps those you counsel could focus on a quality they discovered about themselves during the tragedy or to a part of their body impacted by the event. They could write about their emotions or about what has created their emotional pain. They could write about what confuses them or what brings them pleasure. They could write about what pains them the most or what helps them the most.

How do you answer the question "What do I write?" Whatever they want or whatever comes to mind. Just have them write. Sometimes it helps to have them begin the process in your presence. Again, be sure they write longhand and not use a keyboard.

Once the letter is written, ask them to write a letter back to their grieving or devastated self. Some have actually kept up a written weekly dialogue between the two. Completing this helps the mourner come to grips with what happened to them as well as remembering their life before this occurred. (There is an example of writing a letter to grief in my book *The Complete Guide to Crisis and Trauma Counseling*.)

Another step is to have the Grieving or Devastated Self write to the person years in the future when he or she has stabilized and moved on. After completing this letter, the person can once again respond with a letter from the stabilized self. This is a vital step in helping the mourner realize there is a new life ahead.[12]

Second Step: Facing the Effects of Grief

A second step in helping with the complicated grieving process is facing the effects of the event. We first of all identify the effects—how life has changed because of this death. One way is to list the effects together as you work with the person. You may want to ask the counselee to continue working on the list for the next week in order to recall what isn't accessible to memory at the time you meet. Once everything is listed, identify the most intense affect, then the next, and on and on. Discuss how each effect is manifested in their life, how it's expressed and what it is doing to their life.

If it's helplessness, ask the following:

- Describe *when* your sense of helplessness is the worst.
- Describe *how* it is impacting your daily life.
- When do you not feel helpless?
- What will help you now to overcome your helplessness and move on?
- Who could help you with this, and what would you want them to do?

Exercise—Breathing and Scripture Affirmation
To help those you counsel handle their helpless feelings when you're not around, you could do the following: Ask them to sit and close their eyes. Have them describe the feeling of helplessness in detail. As they do, ask them to raise an index finger if they're beginning to feel helpless. If they do, ask them to breathe in for two and a half seconds and then out for two and a half seconds and repeat this a dozen times. Ask them to repeat these Scriptures aloud several times with the following emphasis:

> I
>> CAN
>>> DO
>>>> ALL
>>>>> THINGS
>>>>>> THROUGH *CHRIST*
>>>>>>> WHO STRENGTHENS ME
>>>>>>> (Phil. 4:13, *NKJV*)

Ask your counselee to describe how he or she feels in regard to helplessness. Suggest that the person do this exercise at home. (I would encourage you to write other scenarios for other effects and experiment with them.)

Every person you minister with needs hope for the present and the future. Perhaps having the person read aloud each day the handout on the following page will help.

Exercise: The Envelope
Another variation of handling the effects of complicated grieving or crippling emotions is "the envelope." In counseling sessions, have these supplies available: paper, a large manila envelope, colored pencil or crayons, and a stapler.

Using colored pencils/markers, ask the person to draw a *symbol* that represents the effect they're struggling with and its feelings, or it could be images or intrusive thoughts. The drawing should be only an abstract

Weathering Life's Storms

On the coast, when residents get a storm warning, they have to prepare. They have to secure lawn furniture or any items that could blow around and injure them. They have to anchor down boats and strap them to something more secure, like the pier. The fierce winds may come, but anchored and securely tied to the strong pier, the boat is still there. This is similar to our hope during the stormy times of grief. You have to remain anchored to those people or beliefs who at that time may be a source of strength. God often chooses to minister to us through other people or His Word. If we do not anchor with the right resources, then we'll be blown apart when these storms hit.

> We have this hope as an anchor for the soul, firm and secure (Heb. 6:19).

> Be strong and let your heart take courage, all you who hope in the Lord (Ps. 31:24, *NASB*).

> Jesus is the same yesterday and today and forever (Heb. 13:8).

Jesus was in your past. He is in your present; He will be in your future. Even though we don't know what will happen to us, Jesus is walking into the future with us. God's love will get us through the toughest of times.

As you integrate this loss into your life, the conflict between your old and new reality continues toward resolution. A sense of peace will emerge. Hope will lead you forward.[13]

symbol and not a drawing of the event(s). Allow no more than five minutes for this drawing.

When the person has completed the drawing, ask him/her to place it inside the manila envelope and seal the envelope.

Hand over a stapler and instruct the person to put as many staples in the envelope as necessary to contain this material for a time when it can be addressed in the future. Allow the person as many staples as he or she wishes. (I've seen some envelopes where staples were all over the envelope.)

Ask the person to write the title of this memory/material on the outside of the envelope, as well as the effect or date.

Tell the person that you will keep this envelope, along with all of its negative thoughts and feelings, secure inside his or her case file. It will remain safely contained there until he or she is ready to work again toward the resolution of this, or when he or she feels that its impact has diminished sufficiently to move on.

Inform your counselees with whom you use "the envelope" exercise that if they think of this issue in the future, they don't have to return to the helpless and overwhelming feelings present during the event itself; instead they can recall that this memory is safe in your office. (I still have one envelope from several years ago.)

Be sure your counselee has gained control before leaving your office. Encourage the client to utilize grounding/self-soothing strategies to regain full control before leaving the office. (One of the best ways is to have the person count backward from 100 by 7s out loud. This moves them from the right side of the brain to the left side. This is an excellent exercise to help engage the hurting side of the brain and reorient them to the present.)[14]

Exercises: Out-of-Control Emotions

There are numerous responses or containment steps that can be used for the effects or for out-of-control emotions. These are important since containment helps the person function each day without being overwhelmed. It provides a way to tolerate intense feelings and choose when he or she wishes to work on them. Containment also helps keep the past separated from the present. Here are a few suggestions.

This approach is the *split screen*. This is similar to watching a television screen where two sports events appear at once. The person divides a mental TV screen, putting the past events on one side and the present on the other. They have remote controls that allow them to mute, slow down, shrink, fast-forward, turn to black and white, or turn off the past. They can download the difficult memories to a videotape while you count from one to three. They turn off the TV, take out the tape, and store or file the tape in a safe place (wherever they want, maybe a safe with a key). Have them place it there until they are ready to take it out again. This provides them with a sense of control.

Freezing is another approach. Have them imagine that the intrusive thoughts, images, feelings, effects or recollections are ice cubes they store at your office. Have them visualize a large scoop that scoops up the ice cubes and drops them into Tupperware containers. Tight-fitting lids on the containers seal in the ice cubes. Have them envision the containers safely stored in a freezer outside your office. Either they or you can retrieve the ice cubes, one container at a time, and use them in an appropriate way to help the therapy progress. Once again this kind of exercise helps them feel more in control.

Another suggestion is the image of *dirty laundry*. Imagine the thoughts, effects, images, feelings or recollections as soiled clothing that needs to go to the laundry. Suggest they see themselves stuffing the soiled clothing in a laundry bag and calling the laundry service. The laundry truck arrives. The laundry bag is placed in the laundry truck, the truck doors are closed and they watch through a window as the laundry truck drives away. Have them watch the truck turn the corner and disappear. The laundry is next to your office. They and you can pick up their laundry together, sort it out and use it in an appropriate way to help their grieving progress.[15]

Fear is a frequent struggle you may encounter with your counselees. One counselee said, "I just don't feel safe anymore. I don't sound rational ever since Tom and his dad were killed. I just can't get it together. I go out on an errand and I don't feel safe. I come home and lock up, and I still don't feel safe. It's like my world changed from safe, secure and solid to unsafe and insecure; and I'm afraid it's always going to be that way."

Fear prevails over this mourner's life. She's dominated by it and she's looking for help, as many are. What would you say or do in this situation? The following is an adapted approach from Dr. Bruce Perry. It's in a narrative form:

It's difficult to go through each day living with such fear. There doesn't seem to be any let-up for you, no safe place at all. Well, let's create one for you that you can go to at any time.

I would like you to sit back and relax. I'd like you to become aware of your breathing. Listen to each breath. Now I would like you to take a number of deep, slow breaths and count them down from ten to one. Every time you exhale imagine that you are taking a step down a staircase. When you get to the bottom of the staircase, there's a door. Reach out, see yourself opening the door and go into this place. Jesus is behind the door: when you see Him you feel His presence and His peace. This is your "safe room" and there is no fear in this room. Now you're in total control here of your thoughts and feelings, and no one, and nothing can hurt you here in this room. Use this when you need to feel safe and to realize that it's possible to live without fear dominating your life.[16]

Hopefully, some of these suggestions about how to help those who are struggling with the effects of complicated grieving or crippling emotions will help you bring healing to those you counsel.

Third Step: Give Order to the Disjointed Pieces

Third, you will need to help the person pull the disjointed thoughts and memories together in some semblance of order. Often mourners will feel as though they're pulled in 20 different directions. They feel disjointed and literally "all over the map," and nothing makes sense to them. Here are some questions to use with counselees to address feelings of disorder and lack of control:

1. It could be you're feeling like a juggler out of control with so much coming at you.
2. Where could we begin to make some sense out of this chaos?
3. What would help you the most at this time? Let's decide together what would help you make sense of this.

Fourth Step: Help Organize the Mourning Process

Fourth, the person needs to mourn but may not know what to begin with or how to mourn. Perhaps helping them identify the various losses and even putting them in categories will help. Revisit the list of secondary losses related to a marriage (see chapter 2). Losses could be material, relational, physical or some even yet to come. Here are questions/statements I've often used:

• It's probably confusing as to "Where do I begin grieving with so many losses?"
• Which of these losses would you prefer grieving over first if that were possible?
• It's difficult to know where to begin grieving. It's even confusing.
• Which of your losses is taking most of your attention?

You may have your own insights and reasons for where a person needs to begin, but you need to see the grief through the person's eyes. He or she may make some bad choices, but these can be corrected. I've found it beneficial to attempt to isolate the losses to avoid being immobilized by the weight of so many.

If you become aware of behavior or reactions that are counterproductive, address them. I have no hesitation in stating that alcohol and medication don't mix, and even to avoid alcohol since it numbs and postpones progress.

Part of our own work is assisting the mourner to acquire new skills and behaviors, or to resurrect those that have been crippled by the death yet still have the potential to be useful. You could say something like this: "I'd be interested in hearing what you were like and what you were capable of doing prior to the death of _____. As we talk about these I'd also like us to consider what you need to learn or acquire in order to move forward in your life. We won't complete this today, but we'll begin. It may be difficult to remember some things at this time, and that's understandable."

It's so common for those who are struggling with complicated grief to feel helpless and powerless. You can create small steps in between the sessions that they are capable of accomplishing and will counter those feelings and ultimately change their perception of themselves. Whatever you can create to help rebuild a positive image will assist in reducing the impact of what they are experiencing. Often it is our ability to see what they are capable of doing that they are incapable of seeing, and it's important to express this to them. You could say:

- I've noticed that you've been able to take care of several items that you felt you were incapable of doing. I'm wondering how you were able to do that. It seems like a large step on your part.

- Have you ever given any thought as to helping others who experience a similar tragedy, at some point in the future? There will be others who will benefit from the insights you have learned through this painful experience.

Another step is helping the mourner come to the place where he or she can recount the experience in a factual manner as if describing it as an event he or she has observed rather than experienced. This would involve being able to piece together all the details, including why and what one was and was not able to do as well as control within the event, and coming to the realization and acceptance of the fact that this event was beyond anyone's capability.

There will be some who have taken on the responsibility for the event as well as the aftermath. Often, blame is transferred to self-blame, which will then create guilt and leave the person stuck in this process.

Mourners will need assistance in learning to relinquish the assumption of responsibility and dealing with survivor guilt. Where this is often difficult is a death by suicide in which the survivors engage in intense self-incrimination: "I could have stopped it . . ." "I should have . . ." "If only . . ." You can use questions or comments such as the following:

- You've been telling me that you feel responsible for this event. It's not unusual for those close to the deceased to feel responsible or want to take responsibility. It may sound strange, but it helps us feel more in control. If you didn't feel responsible, what would your life be like? or What of the following would you be doing differently? or What will it take for you to give up this sense of responsibility?

- It may seem impossible to you right now, but a time will come when you will probably give up feeling this way. If you decide to do this, what would make this happen?

Another step (which can take a long time) is somehow creating meaning out of the event. It will come though searching, questioning, crying, yelling and struggling. Questions or comments like this may help:

- How are you different in both a negative as well as a positive way because of this?
- I know you wish this had never occurred. But it did. Events and losses like this can reinvent us or define us. How do you want to grow because of this?
- What have you learned about yourself so far?

Often I encourage the individual to read Michael Card's book *A Sacred Sorrow*, or David Jeremiah's book *A Bend in the Road*.

You are in the forced process of becoming a new person through this experience, whether you know it or not you're sort of in the driver's seat. You can direct it in an unhealthy way or just the opposite. Which way do you see it going now and which way would you like it to go? How has God been at work in your life during the last few months?[17]

There is so much more we can do for those who mourn. Remember that what is the foundation is a relationship of trust, not technique. Dr. Bruce Perry said, "Relationships are the agents of change, and the most powerful therapy is human love."

CASE STUDY

Jane

This case is a woman in her early fifties who lost her husband in a motorcycle accident four months prior to the beginning of this session.

Jane: When should I start putting away the pictures and stuff . . . I still have the big picture of us together on our wedding day at the service. There's one of him in my room as well as one as a couple.

Counselor: I think you will know when it's time. You will look one day and say, "It's right to put it away."

Jane: Cause we're not a couple anymore . . . [pause]

Counselor: You're not a married woman anymore, but you'll decide. It varies with everyone, and there's no right or wrong time. It's up to you, regardless of what others say.

Jane: I haven't even gone through his clothes yet . . .

Counselor: What do you want to do?

Jane: I don't know. I'm not sure . . . What do others do? It's like there are no guidelines or rules for grief—you know? There's no playbook like in football to follow.

Counselor: Grief makes up its rules as it goes along.

Jane: It's not fair. It's hard enough to get through each day and then to have these—decisions.

Counselor: Grief can be a real pain.

Jane: More than that. [sighs] Well, what about his clothes?

Counselor: What some people do is gradual—some do it all at once. What each person does is right. It's where you're comfortable. Some keep a few items . . . and give away the rest.

Jane: [very softly and intensely] This last week I saw two men that looked exactly like Jim. It was two separate times. One in a store and one on a motorcycle.

Counselor: How did that impact you?

Jane: Oh, it was horrible! I just thought, *Oh, no—No!*

Counselor: Like you couldn't catch your breath?

Jane: Exactly—[pause]

Counselor: It was sort of a shock.

Jane: Oh yeah—it was a real shock . . . of course I wanted to run up to the one getting into the car and say, "Stop!" [laughs]

Counselor: How else did seeing these men impact you?

Jane: It brought back the empty spot in my life and I wanted it filled with him again. It brought up missed feelings, too . . . I wasn't prepared for this happening.

Counselor: You sound like it threw you. This will probably occur again. What could you do to prepare for its occurrence?

Jane: It was like I was thrown from a horse—you know—I don't know . . . I don't know if I could prepare. [pause] The other night I had a really bad nightmare and in it Jim had come back and he was wearing a familiar shirt and he said, "Well, I'm here." And I said, "What do you mean you're here?

Where have you been?" And he said, "I've been traveling all over the world." I asked, "What do you mean?" He replied, "Well, I'm back," as if nothing were wrong. "What do you mean you're back? What have you been doing for nine months?" I yelled. I was so mad at him! Then I woke up after that. I remember at the end I was telling him off . . . "Who do you think you are?" I said, "Who do you think you are to run off and pretend that you're dead then come back into our lives like this? You think that's what you're going to do? You have no idea." I was just livid.

Counselor: It sounds like you're still angry over the way he died— his not listening to your words of caution.

Jane: I guess so. Oh, I was angry.

Counselor: Would you say you're angry at him when you're conscious?

Jane: I thought it was over . . . I really did . . . Wow . . . Yeah, I was angry, and perhaps I still am.

Counselor: It's as though you shocked yourself with the amount of anger within you.

Jane: Yes . . . [pause] I guess I'm wondering where I go from here.

Counselor: Where would you like to go?

Jane: I want to move on—away from anger . . . away from pain.

Counselor: And how can you do that?

Jane: I could remember that I told him how I felt in my dream. I really did . . . there's no reason to tell him again and again. It was good to do that. It felt so real. When I wrote him the letter it was good, but this was better. I felt it . . . I felt he heard me . . . like he hadn't heard me before . . . like he never heard my pleas to quit riding that bike . . . I'd like to let loose of this. As painful and intense as that dream was, I'm glad . . . I don't know when I've had one that felt . . . yes, it felt so real.

Counselor: It's like your dream was a turning point in some way . . . it settled an issue for you so you can move on in your grief.

Jane: Oh, yes, it did.

Analysis

One of the difficult issues to help with are the dreams of those in mourning. It's not unusual for the person to dream that the deceased is alive and then upon waking be hit with the reality that it's not so. Sometimes this reflects a daily conscious struggle.

Sometimes a dream is a reenactment of something that has happened or something they wish for. Dreams can be intermittent or even nightly. The problem often occurs when the mourner asks, "This was my dream. What does it mean?"

Here are some guidelines to follow:

- Ask the person what the dream means to them or what are several possibilities it could mean.
- If the deceased does appear in a dream, it's probably important to the grief process: "What do you think is the significance of what _____ was doing in the dream?"
- Even bits and pieces of dreams when put together can become important.
- If there is a series of dreams, there may be a theme that puts them all together.
- Dreams can occur around significant dates for the mourner. There will be some who would like to dream of the deceased. I've had a number ask when this might occur.

Some dreams move to the realm of nightmare, and those who have experienced trauma may experience some horrific dreams.[18] Dreaming can also help a person face or integrate some of their feelings.

12

Grief Coaching

When you think of a person experiencing grief, what word comes to mind to signify moving out of grief? For many, it's the word "recovery."

There's a new movement and profession that is growing at a rapid rate and has the potential to be useful in ministering to those in grief. It's not counseling; it's coaching. Counseling brings a person from a negative place or experience or difficulty to a place where they are functional and able to cope once again, rather than being limited by their personal problems or experiences. The focus is on identifying their problem and discovering a solution or bringing them to a place of stability. Some refer to this as negative psychology since it focuses on and fixes what's wrong. It's also based upon the counselor, who gives the direction and in a sense is the expert.

Coaching, however, is not centered so much on the counselor but more on the person counseled. You're not re-creating yourself in the other person; you're helping the person in grief discover more of his or her own potential. You're a sounding board for the other person. As one person said, "You are really a thought partner for the griever. You're helping them become accountable to themselves."

Coaching is an equipping type of ministry endeavoring to move a person from where they are to where they *want to be* in their life. It's more than counseling. It's more than recovery. Dr. Gary Collins describes it in this way: "Coaching helps people expand their visions, build their confidence, unlock their potential, increase their skills and take practical steps toward their goals. Unlike counseling or therapy, coaching is less threatening, less concerned about problem solving and more inclined to help people reach their potentials."[1] Coaching is also about helping people grow on their own, not because you told them what and how to do it.

There is accountability in the coaching relationship, but it's unique since it is judgment free. The emphasis is on learning rather than results. A grief coach does not need to be right, but only to assist.

The Key Components of a Coaching Ministry

The first step in building an effective coaching relationship is to create a safe and courageous space for the person. We use the word "courageous" purposely here because, although as coaches we can be encouraging, counselees need to find the courage in themselves to make significant change in their lives. After all, if what they want was easy to accomplish, they would already be doing it. They wouldn't need a coach or the coaching relationship. The environment that is created must be safe enough for counselees to take the risks they need to take and be courageous. It is in this space that counselees will be able to approach their lives with curiosity, interest, power, creativity and choice.[2]

Some refer to it as Positive Psychology, and it is future-oriented to help individuals move to a higher level of fulfillment. It could be that coaching is something new for you. It's not a fad but has become an accepted way of helping others and has created a multitude of new professions. Some that may be most familiar are life coaching and career coaching. But there's also business coaching, church coaching, corporate coaching, executive coaching, marriage and parenting coaching, relationship coaching, just to mention a few. And remember, its emphasis is not on problems but on solutions.

A Coach Is an Encourager

Coaching has a great deal to do with being an encourager and helping a person develop his or her potential, some of which the person may not even be aware of at this time.

To be an encourager you need to have an attitude of optimism. The *American Heritage Dictionary* has one of the better definitions of the word "optimist." It's a "tendency or disposition to expect the best possible outcome, or to dwell on the most hopeful aspect of a situation." When this is your attitude or perspective, you'll be able to encourage others. Encouragement is "to inspire; to continue on a chosen course, to impart courage or confidence."

Encouragement is freely given. It can involve noticing something in a person that others take for granted, and affirming something that others notice but may never think of mentioning.

John Maxwell, in his book *Be a People Person,* says we need to anticipate that others will do their best. "When working with people I always try to look at them not as they are but as what they can be. By anticipating that vision will become real, it's easy for me to encourage them as they stretch. Raise your anticipation level, and you raise their achievement level."[3]

In Acts 18:27, the word "encourage" means "to urge forward or persuade." In 1 Thessalonians 5:11, it means "to stimulate another person to the ordinary duties of life." Consider the words found in 1 Thessalonians 5:14: "And we earnestly beseech you, brethren, admonish (warn and seriously advise) those who are out of line [the loafers, the disorderly and the unruly]; encourage the timid and fainthearted, help and give your support to the weak souls [and] be very patient with everybody [always keeping your temper]" (*AMP*).

Scripture uses a variety of words to describe both our involvement with others as well as the actual relationships. "Urge" (*parakaleo*) means "to beseech or exhort." It is intended to create an environment of urgency to listen and respond to a directive. It is a mildly active verb. Paul used it in Romans 12:1 and in 1 Corinthians 1:4.

The word "encourage" (*paramutheomai*) means "to console, comfort and cheer up." This process includes elements of understanding, redirecting of thoughts and a general shifting of focus from the negative to the positive. In the context of the verse, it refers to the timid ("fainthearted," *KJV*) individual who is discouraged and ready to give up. It's a matter of loaning your faith and hope to the person until his or her own develops.

The word "help" (*anechomai*) primarily contains the idea of "taking interest in, being devoted to, rendering assistance, or holding up spiritually and emotionally." It is not so much an active involvement as a passive approach. It suggests the idea of coming alongside a person and supporting him. In the context of 1 Thessalonians 5:14, it seems to refer to those who are incapable of helping themselves.

Coaching is helping a person move forward and discover a new way of living that may even surprise them. As a grief coach you are a resource for the person's self-reflection. Your role is to help the person being coached see what they can't see for themselves. Listening, clarifying, reflecting, asking are part of the process. It's not figuring out what to do; it's them. Just like counseling, it involves working ourselves out of a job. Another perspective is once the person being coached moves from A to B, he continues the coaching process to discover and name what C looks like, and keeps moving forward.

Right about now you may be saying, "But that's what I've been doing all along. I've used that approach and those questions for years!" It almost sounds like giving a style of counseling a new name—"coaching." There can be an overlap between the two and even a blending of a counseling style and a coaching style. I realized I've been doing this for the last 30 years myself. Often as individuals or couples came for counseling and wanted to discuss their problems or what wasn't working in their marriage, I would shift to discover what was working, what was going well and then focus on what they could do to reach their personal or relational potential. The questions I've often used are the questions used in coaching.

Coaching's focus is not just to bring a person back to where they were but to help them discuss what they can do to move beyond and function at a new level. When you function as a coach, you're a team. You *stand next to* the person. You *help* discover what they can do; you guide and encourage. The person you're ministering to may not believe that, but this is part of our task. You're not a direct advice giver. Your assumption is that the other person is the one who has the ability to determine and discover what he or she can do to move forward in life. Our belief in their ability and potential will help them catch the vision. The author of *Leadership Coaching* said, "When I'm coaching, I'm pushing a person to draw from his or her own resources and experiences. Coaching is helping people learn instead of teaching them."[4]

One of the goals for someone in grief is helping him or her design their new future. For a person in grief to be able to come to the place of believing there is a future is a positive first step.

Just as in the counseling process, there will be setbacks and regression in the coaching process. Personal expectations may need to be visited and revised so they are realistic. But there is another reason for progress to be interrupted. The authors of *Co-Active Coaching* refer to it as the Gremlin Effect. This is the person's inner voice or self-talk, which can cripple moving forward. The self-talk tends to be self-critical and negative. It may question the possibility of change or that changes won't last. Whenever risk is involved the voice may appear, and it uses words and phrases like "should," "shouldn't," "can't," "isn't," "I don't," and so on. Gremlins are there to point out weaknesses, fear and failures and to reinforce self-limiting judgments. Gremlins want to hold back progress.

Ask questions like, "As we work together and we begin to make progress, what thoughts might come to mind that would hold you back or derail your moving forward?" Asking this early can be helpful so the person being coached is able to address when it happens and realize that this is normal.[5] Remember, this is not therapy or counseling. It's the art of asking significant questions to help people grow and move to where they and God want them to be in their life. It's helping others discover what God can be doing in their lives as well. Dr. Gary Collins describes it in this way: "In working with others, coaching helps people clarify their calling, discover their vision, and take steps to reach the goals God appears to have put in their lives."[6]

One of the newest applications of the coaching world is grief coaching. Is it applicable? Can it work, especially when you understand the dynamics and upheaval of the grief process? For many, just surviving daily existence is an overload, let alone moving to a new level of positive functioning.

Grief coaching uses some of the same methodology as grief counseling for it to be successful. Focused listening is at the heart of both so you can clarify issues and develop an accurate understanding of the person's life, issues and dreams. One of the qualities that is vital in being a successful coach is curiosity:

> For coaching, curiosity may be the quality that starts the process and the energy that keeps it going. The most effective coaches seem to be naturally curious and to have developed their curiosity in a way that opens doors and windows for clients . . . Authentic curiosity is a powerful builder of relationships.[7]

The Language of Coaching

As a grief coach, there are numerous words you use in your interactions and questions with your counselee.

- What do you think would work for you this next week?
- What have you done before that has worked for you?
- What have you tried that you wouldn't try again?
- What is your best way of reaching your goals?
- What might keep you from reaching your goal?

You're looking for ways the person would like to change. Remember that a person in grief might vacillate between wanting to change and grow and not believing he/she is capable of doing so.

There are good questions and there are poorly stated questions in coaching. Consider the following areas to avoid.

Closed questions—These tend to inhibit the person. Closed questions are those that can be answered with a "yes" or "no" and don't encourage creative thinking. Adding the words "what" or "how" will help.

A subtle type of closed question is when you ask for a solution but you're actually giving advice that is your own solution. These are questions that begin with "Should you, could you, can you, will you," and so on. "You" is the key word to avoid.

Rambling questions are when you ask the same question in different ways and perhaps even throw in some potential answers at the same time. If the person being coached doesn't understand the question, let them tell you.

Interpretive questions are those responses that put your own interpretation on what they said. As much as possible it's best to use their own words in your question, which shows you hear what they're saying. In coaching we echo/parrot back verbatim. Hearing what they're saying is helpful for the person being coached and keeps coaches from making assumptions or suggestions about what the person thinks or means.

Rhetorical questions are not really questions but statements reflecting your own opinion while remaining somewhat hidden. These usually reflect the fact that you've made a judgment of some kind.

Leading questions are those that point the person to the solution you think is best, not their solutions. An example is, "You've said you experienced a lot of emotions this week. Would you call it depression?" rather than listing several emotions or asking, "How would you label the emotions you've experienced this week?"

One of the questions we avoid in coaching is "Why?" It's not only difficult to answer, but it can also keep a person from moving toward and focusing on the future. They might slip into talking about the past or excuses or may become defensive. It's best to limit yourself to asking questions that begin with "What?" "When?" "How?" "Who?" or "Where?" But be sure that your questions ask for more than a "yes" or "no" response. You want your questions to cause people to think, to learn to respond out of the left side of the brain. You want them to look at and consider things they've not considered before.

Here are some examples:

- What would moving out of your grief look like to you?
- What are some steps you could take to make that a reality?
- How will you keep yourself focused on doing that?
- What might get in the way of following through?

- Who is there in your life that you can count on to help you?
- Tell me what you have learned in your grief state that will help you in the future.
- How will you measure whether you're progressing in your grief journey?
- When we face a crisis or suffering we have several responses. We can be broken by it, survive it or grow through the experience. What could you do to be able to grow from this?
- What fears or obstacles might be keeping you from moving on at this time in your grief? What steps could be taken to overcome these? Imagine it's 10 years from now; what would you like to tell others about this time in your life?[8]

A counselor from many years ago said, "Don't ask random, aimless questions. Ask questions that have substance to them, questions that help clients get somewhere. Ask questions that challenge the client to think."[9] Some of the questions are for clarification and some are for action.

Whether you're counseling or coaching, how you respond to how people answer is critical. Our answers need to show that we're really listening. Using their language and style of speaking is essential. Every chance you get to do so, encourage and affirm their decisions. Believe in them and their ability to move beyond their grief. Lend them your hope.

Coaching is future and positive oriented. When you're grieving there's little energy and ability to focus on a bright new future. It seems unbelievable and unattainable. We need to honor and respect where each person is and work slowly on focusing them away from their grief and onto the future. Don't get bogged down in talking about what isn't working or why it isn't working. Use time and energy on creating what will work.

There is a delicate balance of moving from normalizing and educating during the early stages of grief into a coaching process.

Perhaps this diagram will help to explain the process:

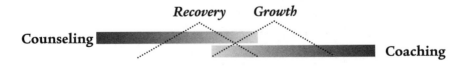

As you can see, you don't begin with coaching. As you move along, and the person progresses toward recovery, coaching overlaps and is slowly brought into the process. Eventually this coaching model becomes more prominent until it's your main approach. Is there a time frame for this? No one can give you one since it's difficult to capture and identify the timing of the grief process. With some they're ready in a few weeks, while with many it will be months and years. Another factor is whether it was a sudden death, a complicated grief or whether the pain is instrumental or intuitive grieving, and so on.

Grief Coaching Questions to Ask

1. What would be helpful for us to work on today?
2. What would you like to talk about today?
3. How would you describe your grief during the past week?
4. How would you like to respond to your grief differently this next week?
5. How will you accomplish this?
6. When are the times when your grief isn't as intense?
7. Let's imagine that your grief has subsided and you're experiencing life again. What would this look like?
8. Describe your life having recovered from grief and learning from the experience. What would this be like?
9. If you were able to move ahead this week, what would you do?
10. What abilities do you have that perhaps you're not using that will help you move on?
11. How will you overcome your tendency to stay where you are?
12. What do you want to be able to do a year from now?
13. Often in grief, our dreams of the future die. What would you like to resurrect?
14. What did you believe about grief before the death of _____ _____, and what do you believe now?

15. What did you believe about God before the death of _____
    _____, and what do you believe now?
16. Where would you like to be in your grief 90 days from now?
    Six months from now? One year from now? Five years from
    now (and so on)?
17. What will you do to make that happen?
18. Where would you like to be five years from now in your rela-
    tionship with God?
19. What will you do to make that happen?

This chapter is simply an introduction to the new field of grief
coaching. I'm sure that in the near future there will be books and other
practical resources that will take the ministry to a new level. If you are interested in learning more about coaching, please read the following as a
beginning step:

- *Christian Counseling*, Dr. Gary Collins (Thomas Nelson, 2007).
- *Coaching Questions: A Coach's Guide to Powerful Asking Skills*, Tony
  Stoltzfus (Pegasus, 2008).
- *Co-Active Coaching: New Skills for Coaching People Toward Success in
  Work and Life*, Laura Whitworth, Karen Kimsey-House, Henry
  Kimsey-House and Phillip Sandohl (Davies-Black Publishing,
  1998).
- *Complete Guide to Christian Coach Training*. For more information
  on ordering, please go to www.christiancoachingresources.com.

For information on training as a grief coach, go to www.griefcoach
ingcenter.com.

Verbatim Transcripts of Actual Counseling Sessions

The cases contained in this chapter are transcripts of live counseling sessions, some of which occurred in front of a graduate class. All were videotaped and, upon the conclusion of the session, were discussed and analyzed by the class members. One of the best ways to learn to counsel is to observe live counseling or to read actual transcripts, which is why so many have been included in this book. The counselor's responses reflect his style and manner and theory of counseling and are not the only way to respond. There are other statements or questions that could be used to respond to the counselee just as effectively or even more so.

Hopefully, these cases will provide you with a better feel for grief counseling and various ways to respond. After you read chapter 12 on grief coaching, return to these cases to see if the interaction was coaching or counseling or a blend of the two.

After each session, write down what you learned and what you might have done or said differently. Try to imagine the tone of voice the counselor used in the sessions.

In what way do you see the counselor connecting with and coming alongside the counselee?

CASE STUDY

Eve

Counselor: I'll let you begin where you're comfortable, Eve.

Eve: This is a bit of a recent loss. [pause] On November 5, I lost a very, very close friend. It was from the swine flu. It was a very sudden loss, unexpected. And we had recently had a disagreement. So I blame myself. Somehow I felt responsible, so that made it harder, because I wasn't there to encourage proper medical care and that sort of thing. [speaking slowly and softly]

Counselor: So you're taking on some real responsibility for this person's death.

Eve: Yes . . . yes.

Counselor: And what was this person's name.

Eve: His name was Warren.

Counselor: Warren.

Eve: And he didn't go to the doctor soon enough, and I felt like that was the reason that he died. So it's been very difficult. I can't . . . I know logically I'm not responsible, but internally I was thinking, I keep telling myself, "If only this . . ." I reenacted making contact in time to say, "Oh, are you sick? You should go to the doctor."

Counselor: So your mind is telling you one thing, but your heart seems to be overriding that and you're taking on that responsibility? [tentatively]

Eve: I am.

Counselor: And when you reenact this in your mind, how does that leave you?

Eve: Oh, I feel terrible. I feel so guilty. I feel lost and sad. I started to get migraine headaches. I realized I was punishing myself each time I'd think it.

Counselor: How long did you know Warren?

Eve: Probably 32 years.

Counselor: So it was a long relationship.

Eve: A long friendship . . . very long friendship. Very long . . . [voice trails off]

Counselor: And you're thinking, "If we hadn't had this rift, then I could have saved him."

Eve: Right, I had tried to get back in touch but by then I didn't know he was sick. I actually heard about it accidentally. Someone who knew I knew him said, "You know Warren's in ICU; how's he doing?" I said, "Oh, I don't know." I was in shock; I couldn't believe he'd been there for 17 days before I heard. And he was all alone during his illness part. So, I waited to go to the doctor to the last minute and it was too late.

Counselor: You're thinking, "I could have prevented this from happening."

Eve: Yeah, I think that over and over and over. And I know he probably wouldn't have even listened to me. He was a very stubborn person, very stubborn, because his son was living with him, and he wouldn't listen to anybody.

Counselor: So there were other people who probably encouraged him to go to the doctor.

Eve: Probably

Counselor: But he didn't listen to them.

Eve: Well, actually just his son. He never let anyone at work know how bad he was, how sick he was. They just kept thinking he would be coming back next week. One of his co-workers, she felt guilty too because she was with him when she dropped him off, and she knew how sick he was. But she didn't have the kind of connection with him that she would call. Well, she got sick herself from the swine flu. And it's been since November; it's a little better, but suddenly it will come over me.

Counselor: It's still heavy on your heart.

Eve: It's so heavy; it's so painful.

Counselor: But you're not certain he would have listened to you.

Eve: No, honestly I know he probably wouldn't have. He's very stubborn about going to the doctor about anything.

Counselor: Like many men.

Eve: Yes, like many men. [smiles]

Counselor: But still, because of that connection you just wish, "I could have done something to help him."

Eve: I feel so helpless. This is the worst part though. I never say anything to anybody. He had sort of a sharp way of saying things. It was part of him; everybody knew that. And I never said anything back. And this one time it was over something stupid. He made a comment about my car. I carry all my files. And he made some comment. And I said, "I don't ever want to talk to you." But it was a lot of things. I said, "I don't want to talk to you anymore." It hurt my feelings.

Counselor: It sounds like it was a build-up; it wasn't just what happened then.

Eve: So I said, "I never want to talk to you again." I didn't really mean it, because I never say that to anyone. But then I thought he probably really believes it. So, then I was afraid to call him back. We didn't speak ever again. It was so hard. I feel like he left the earth thinking I never wanted to talk to him again. He was such a good friend.

Counselor: You had a lot of good times together.

Eve: We worked in a lot of different places together. He was a very great person. Just didn't like to go to the doctor. I felt so helpless.

Counselor: It sounds like you still have some things you'd like to say to him. Have you written him a letter?

Eve: No, I haven't. It's an idea.

Counselor: Do you think it would help?

Eve: Yeah, I think it would.

Counselor: If you were to write it, what would you do with it?

Eve: Oh, I'd probably read it out loud. That would probably help.

Counselor: Where would you read this?

Eve: I just heard they are getting ready to get his headstone ready. Maybe I could read it at his grave. It's funny because I've been thinking about what to do to go there . . . what would I do? In Judaism you leave stones to show that you have been there. And I was reading about it last night, you know, like an altar. I have a stone from Israel. It's a tradition that comes from many different places. And I have a stone that I have from when I went to Israel. He always said he wanted to go to Israel for the history. He didn't have any belief system at all, in God. [takes a Kleenex] That would be a healing thing to read the letter.

Counselor: What would you like to say?

Eve: Just to thank him for being such a good friend. To tell him I miss him and that a lot of people miss him. He was such a beloved person. To tell him I wish he hadn't been so stubborn, but we know that was who he was. Just to put those feelings into words, give words to those feelings.

Counselor: Churning. They're churning around a lot inside of you, aren't they?

Eve: Just even talking I feel some relief. They come back. It seems that they come back all of a sudden.

Counselor: You also alluded to regrets. I wonder what you could do about the regrets.

Eve: Well, I think the one thing was the regret. I rarely even speak to somebody if they have a bad temper—I think I won't talk to them for a while. And to make sure I never leave a friend without making sure that we're still connected. Never say I won't ever talk to you again. I don't know why I said that.

Counselor: This is becoming sort of a learning experience?

Eve: To learn how important every moment is. And not to lose a chance to do some healing. And to make sure we reconnect with each other even when we've been upset in a moment. Never walk away from anyone whether I care about them or not, like Warren. Every person is important who comes in my path. I don't want to ever regret the thing about words. Not to put words out that are going to hurt. I do regret that. Because you don't know if you're ever going to see that person again. You just don't know!

Counselor: And you really don't fully know how he felt toward you after that either. I guess we all tend to assume the worst.

Eve: Oh, yes.

Counselor: Can you think of anything else you might be able to do that can help you at this time?

Eve: I think talking about this here and writing the letter. I need to reconnect with the woman who was with him when he got ill because she carried so much guilt, too, because she didn't go back and reconnect with him. We've formed a bond and friendship together and because of that we can both share together. That's been very helpful.

Counselor: The situation itself where you had the altercation with him, does it play over sometimes in your mind?

Eve: Yes.

Counselor: I imagine when that happens it's still pretty upsetting.

Eve: It still hurts.

Counselor: What do you think about writing that out in detail in longhand?

Eve: Oh, I hadn't thought of that. I have such rare altercations . . . Yeah, that would be good, because it's painful to think about.

Counselor: Sometimes those thoughts get stuck on a circular loop and they keep playing. And one of the best ways is it's just best to write it.

Eve: I like that idea. [pause] Yes, that would be good.

Counselor: Can you think of anything else you might be able to do?

Eve: Well, one of the things I am doing . . . that's why I'm taking this class, is because I want to be able to help others. I've counseled for a long time but feel like I went right through the fire with this loss. I lost my dad 11 years ago . . . that was hard, and I've had the miscarriages . . . that was hard. Maybe part of this is I'm feeling I should have known. I'm mad at myself as a counselor; I should have known to do this differently. Just to give myself permission to be human, not to expect myself to know everything when I'm in a situation like this.

Counselor: To be a bit more accepting of yourself.

Eve: Forgiving. To find some forgiveness for myself, that's important.

Counselor: Very important. And we know who does forgive us, don't we? Well, thank you for being brave enough to sit here with us.

Analysis

As you look back over this session, you can see that Eve gave a synopsis of her struggle in the initial paragraph. A serious sudden loss, a broken relationship, self-blame and overly responsible.

The counselor reflected back or summarized what she appeared to be experiencing and personalized the session by obtaining Warren's name. As the session continued, Eve filled in the details that clarified why she was so upset. This is why it's so important that we create a setting in which they can tell their story and perhaps share it again and again.

Midway through the session we shifted from reflecting and summarizing to what she could do, and we were specific. Would writing a letter help? What would you do with it? Where to read it? What would you say? Bring up questions so there is more chance of follow-through. A possibility to consider discussing at a later session would be the death of her father and her miscarriages.

The following are some of the statements and questions the counselor used. What do you notice about the style of the questions and comments?

- So you're taking on some real responsibility for this person's death.
- So your mind is telling you one thing, but your heart seems to be overriding that and you're taking on that responsibility?
- When you reenact this in your mind, how does that leave you?
- So it was a long relationship.
- And you're thinking, "If we hadn't had this rift, then I could have saved him."
- You're thinking, "I could have prevented this from happening."
- So there were other people who probably encouraged him to go to the doctor.
- It's still heavy on your heart.
- But you're not certain he would have listened to you.
- It sounds like it was a build-up—it wasn't just what happened then.
- You had a lot of good times together.
- It sounds like you still have some things you'd like to say to him. Have you written him a letter?
- If you were to write it, what would you do with it?
- Where would you read this?
- What would you like to say?
- You also alluded to regrets. I wonder what you could do about the regrets.
- This is becoming sort of a learning experience?
- And you really don't fully know how he felt toward you after that either. I guess we all tend to assume the worst.
- Can you think of anything else you might be able to do that can help you at this time?
- The situation itself where you had the altercation with him— do you still play it over sometimes in your mind?
- I imagine when that happens it's still pretty upsetting.
- What do you think about writing that out in detail in long-hand?
- Can you think of anything else you might be able to do?

Questions

1. What did you learn from this session?
2. What would you do differently?

CASE STUDY

John

Counselor: I'll let you begin wherever you feel comfortable, John.

John: My name is Chaplain John and I had a mission failure this week. [pause] Part of my job as a chaplain is to share Jesus with everyone that I meet. And I met a fellow whose belief system was so different than mine that I was speechless. I didn't know what to say. I was at a loss. I left that encounter just by saying, "I hope God blesses you in a special way." But I've never encountered that situation before and it's bothered me ever since.

Counselor: [pause] Did you give any thought to what you wish you might have said?

John: I'm still at a loss.

Counselor: Are you?

John: Yeah. His belief system was kind of like Voltaire's "I think, therefore I am." I think it was Voltaire. He stated he was dying of lung cancer and he stated that life exists because he thinks he does. And that [pause] if I believed that Jesus was God, that was good for me but that's not the way he believed. Last year, I lost at least seven biker friends, including one of my very closest friends. If I don't share Jesus with people, I recall how short life is. And I just felt inadequate. I didn't feel like I'd failed, but I felt like I was not prepared. I don't want to be in that position again. I want to be prepared for everything that I can be prepared for. And that was just one that . . .

I can talk to a Muslim, I can talk to a Shinto, I can talk to almost any other religion, but had not come across someone who rejected religion. He wasn't an atheist; he just was foreign to my experience.

Counselor: So this has been weighing heavily on your mind.

John: More heavily than I thought it would. Yes.

Counselor: What are some of the thoughts that you've had about yourself after this encounter?

John: I've been disappointed in myself that I wasn't prepared. I thought maybe I hadn't read the Scriptures with enough discernment. [long pause] I'm disappointed in myself.

Counselor: So even though you've never run into this before, you still feel as though, "I should have been able to handle this."

John: Yes, exactly. [pause] I don't want to be able not to handle it in the future. This was a learning experience for me. I don't want to let an opportunity to go by because I'm not prepared.

Counselor: John, if you were to go back and encounter him at this time, have you given any thought to what you would say?

John: I have, and I still don't know what I would . . . what I should say. And that troubles me. I still don't have an answer, even now.

Counselor: You've said this is something you haven't run into before, and not really heard before.

John: I heard it in college.

Counselor: But not . . .

John: Not in real life.

Counselor: I wonder what would happen if you reflected that to him. "This is different. I've not run into this before."

John: [thinking] That would be better than what I did do.

Counselor: Okay. [pause] Everything that we encounter that we wish would be different we have an opportunity to learn.

John: Well, I thought of our first class when you said no matter how well we're trained, no matter how much we read, no matter how experienced we are, we will run into situations that we've never encountered before.

Counselor: This was it. [nodding]

John: And this was mine. I am a very compassionate person, but I'm also a very controlled person. The fact that I couldn't handle this, I didn't know what to say, kind of knocked one of my legs out from under me, emotionally, I guess.

Counselor: It really sounds like it threw you in some ways.

John: It did. I've been a chaplain for three years and I've counseled with a lot of people, been through a lot of things, but this was just one I was ill equipped for.

Counselor: What comes to mind is when we talked about the losses, where you're experiencing one of those, where you weren't exactly who you thought you were.

John: Yeah, I kind of lost a little bit of my self-esteem.

Counselor: A little bit of your confidence?

John: Yes. And that's not a good place for me to be. I know all the things that I would tell people. God loves me. I'm going to heaven. God called me to be a chaplain. In a future situation my confidence has been shaken a little bit. I've been praying about it, reading Scripture and would like to get that confidence back.

Counselor: What do you think you could do to regain that?

John: Partly what I'm doing right now. [little bit of laughter] It's been a difficult thing to share. People that aren't involved with ministering to other people wouldn't have a clue.

Counselor: They wouldn't understand. It sounds like you're quite brave though to be this open in front of a group.

John: My need to discuss it is greater than my fear of being up here with you. [more laughter] I do appreciate you doing this. I think for me just getting it out in front of others is very helpful. Because now it is not inside me all by myself dealing with it.

Counselor: All the rest of us can carry this around and pray for you too.

John: Definitely. [nodding]

Counselor: Because I think all of us can identify with you. You've had a very hard situation because you think, "Where do I go with this? What do I say?"

John: I can tell you I am actually feeling a physical sense of relief right now. I feel better. Thank you.

Counselor: You're welcome.

John: [deep breath and pause]

Counselor: I imagine in the future after this class you'll think, "Well, maybe I could have said this, or maybe I could say this next time." Build some more phrases within you. It could be this gentleman will not be the last.

John: I don't imagine he will be. That's why I'm really looking forward to completing this class.

Counselor: You know, I'm glad you're here. I wanted to pick up on something else you said, John. You said you lost seven bikers in the last year.

John: And five the year before that.

Counselor: And one was very close?

John: One was one of my closest friends.

Counselor: And how are you handling that?

John: [choking back tears] I miss him.

Counselor: I'm feeling your pain right now.

John: My wife led him to the Lord. I was out of town and she called me and said that he wanted to accept Jesus and what should she do? [laughter] And I told her over the phone and she did that. And I know where he is.

Counselor: What was his name?

John: Ted

Counselor: Ted.

John: I did his funeral, I did his wife's funeral, and I did his father's funeral. [struggling] Five funerals all have been part of that group.

Counselor: You still miss him very much.

John: Yes, and his wife who was also a very close friend of mine too. The couple who were head of the Bakersfield Toy Run died last year. They were close personal friends of mine. I'm on the Toy Run Committee.

Counselor: Yes. [acknowledging his losses and encouraging him to go on]

John: [pause] I'm pretty well self-contained, and I haven't got it all out of my system yet.

Counselor: You have a lot of complicated grief there, because you've had one after another. And it's hard to grieve for so many.

John: I started attending GriefShare because I was having trouble coping. With Pastor Steve, and that was helpful. But I recognize that I haven't got it all out of my system yet and probably won't for a while. But during all of that and dealing with all of that I've had to minister to others. And go through the struggle with my own dealing with my own issues and putting them aside and counseling others. And there are times that I just run out of John. And so I'm really looking forward to learning a lot in this class.

Counselor: I think everybody here, John, feels with you and identifies with you because we all struggle with our stuff while ministering to others. We run out of John or Norm, and then we go to the Lord.

John: Amen. That's where I go. I have a prayer partner, an accountability partner.

Counselor: Have you ever given any thought to writing a goodbye letter to your friend?

John: I have thought about it, but I haven't done it yet.

Counselor: It's something to think about.

John: [pause, nodding] I probably should.

Counselor: Thank you for your transparency.

John: You're welcome. Thank you.

Analysis

The counselee was quite articulate and introspective with a deep commitment to minister to others. Look at each of the counselor's responses and decide which part of what John said that he's responding to. Why did he say what he said? The counselor's responses were often tentative, and varied from reflective comments to questions—the session began with more of a cognitive emphasis and then shifted to the emotions. It's important to clarify and talk about other losses alluded to in a conversation, and in this case, it was his seven friends.

Questions

1. What did you learn from this session?
2. What would you do differently?

— CASE STUDY —

Carol

Counselor: What brings you in, Carol?

Carol: My oldest adopted child, who is now living in a placement home out of state. One of the big losses I can't stop grieving is his losses. He was abandoned at seven months and left in a crib until he was six years old. He just got out of diapers at 17. I think I'm grieving my kid's losses. I just found out about a significant sexual abuse incident with my younger son in an orphanage that he's been carrying around, and I'm just trying to make up for what they missed. I'm not able to, and I'm feeling hopeless. Before Jimmy was taken out of state, he became very violent. He broke up the house. And in the middle of all that I found out that my new husband had been lying to me, and I couldn't trust him anymore. I'm not sure where I am in the grieving process. I'm doing a lot of work. I'm trying to process all this. I'm wondering who I can trust. My trust has been shattered. This is on top of feeling responsible for my sons. And my oldest son is now in the care of other people. It's hard to have your child being cared for in out-of-home care, and it's hard because you're not sure if they're going to be abused again. My youngest son who is blind told me about this abuse right before I put him on a bus to go to a boarding school. So they are both being cared for by other people that I don't necessarily trust. So I'm really feeling hopeless.

Counselor: You're really on overload. Grieving the losses of your children that they've experienced, grieving the loss of your children and the loss of your dreams for your marriage. So it's like, "Where do I go from here? What can I do? Who can I trust?"

Carol: I'm trying to set an example of faith for my youngest one. He has such a heart for God, but he's now watching the man who said he would be his father betray him. Of course, this triggers the loss of my own father leaving.

Counselor: Abandonment.

Carol: I'm learning to separate incidences and grieve losses separately. This is this one . . . and this is this one . . . But it' seems like I've been in a state of constant crisis because of this thing with Jimmy.

Counselor: You're still in a crisis state now, pretty much.

Carol: It feels like it.

Counselor: Have you numerated your losses?

Carol: I did a date line thing in Bible study, and it doesn't look very good on paper.

Counselor: One of the ways you can begin to work on this is to segment it. Just take one or two of the losses away from it and put those down. And then you can focus on those losses without everything else coming in like a flood and overwhelming you. And that way you can feel like you have a better handle on it. Have you tried that?

Carol: No, I haven't.

Counselor: Probably give that a try. Because with everything I know about you before now, this is like an overload—it's just too much. But this way you can just take a chunk at a time. Now, how are you grieving these losses? What do you do to grieve them?

Carol: I'm not journaling like I should, I know that.

Counselor: So that's helped before.

Carol: I'm at home alone more during the week with Tommy gone, so I'm having more out-loud conversations with God.

Counselor: Has that been helpful?

Carol: It's been helpful. I eat more, that's not been helpful.

Counselor: All right. As you're praying, are you writing some prayers?

Carol: I feel like it's kind of stuck in there.

Counselor: How do you get it unstuck?

Carol: We start writing.

Counselor: Okay. Is that part of your plan, to do that? Would you like to do that?

Carol: Yes.

Counselor: Who else do you have in your life that you trust that can come up and walk alongside you and listen to you and walk with you?

Carol: I have many good, solid friends who are walking with me.

Counselor: So you have a support team?

Carol: I do.

Counselor: And you're using them?

Carol: Yes. I feel like most of the people that are close to me and counsel me tell me I'm doing the right thing. There's a huge load of guilt when it comes to my marriage. I've asked him to leave. I'm not sure whose eyes I am looking through when

I look in the mirror, but it's not the people who are counseling me. So I feel a lot more condemnation than I would like to feel.

Counselor: You're allowing condemning thoughts to reside in you rather than, "This is the best, this is the healthiest, this is the best thing to do."

Carol: But I'm the oldest child. And I'm the strong one, overly responsible.

Counselor: So you're responsible. Firstborn and stuff. Why don't we write down those condemning thoughts and balance them out with all the good reasons and possible reasons.

Carol: [nodding in agreement]

Counselor: Now, you're a reader, I know that. In the book *Feeling Good: New Mood Therapy*, by David Burns, there's an excellent chapter on guilt. This might help you in the process of relinquishing that part. Because when you can see one little part of your life beginning to balance out, that's the seed for hope in some of the other areas. So do you think that's something you could do?

Analysis

This is a complicated loss situation because of so many ongoing loss situations, including ambiguous as well as disenfranchised losses. The ongoing issues make it difficult to find any closure, so helping her develop coping skills is important. The constant mental concern could easily feed ongoing worry as well as develop an anxiety state. With multiple losses, break them down one by one so they're manageable. Another possibility is showing the Crisis Sequence Chart from chapter 8. Carol was already aware of the chart and could place herself within it and knew that what she was experiencing was normal. Toward the end, I became a bit more directive in terms of writing, prayer, support from others and reading. It's important to encourage counselees to take positive steps during the week to continue growing, and reading is at the top of the list.

Police Officer

A 54-year-old retired police officer came for his twelfth session of grief counseling. His wife of 20 years had died after 18 years of a blood disorder and cancer. The counselee has struggled to move forward, and his progress has been consistent and gradual. For weeks he felt he would always be in the depth of his grief and his life would never change. Even the activities he forced himself to engage in held no meaning for him. He did attend a Grief-Share for several weeks. Very gradually he is admitting to moving forward.

Counselor: How have the last two weeks been for you?

Jim: Oh . . . so-so, the same as always. [expressionless tone of voice]

Counselor: What has been different or better for you?

Jim: Well, I've only cried two days this week instead of every day, and uh, I've been writing about Jan.

Counselor: So, there have been some major differences.

Jim: Yeah—I guess there has after all. The writing—you suggested to write just 10 minutes at a time, but I've been writing for an hour and then correct it while I remember something new. Otherwise, I'd forget. I've written about three pages overall.

Counselor: You've done more than you imagined.

Jim: I guess I have.

Counselor: What has the experiencing of writing about Jan been like for you?

Jim: Well, it's memories, you know, memories of her and us, and it's painful . . . really painful to write about them—to revisit, but I'm committed to do this. I guess it's helping to drain what was stuck in there. And, as you said, I'm capturing memories I'm likely to forget in the future.

Counselor: It seems that even though you're facing your pain, there's a benefit to it.

Jim: I guess so . . . [long pause] You know, I went to visit my brother-in-law again this past week. They're gracious and everything. I just called and invited myself over, which is all right with them, but I got the feeling I was in the way. It's as though people are tired of having me around. It's been almost a year, about 10 months, that I've been alone now, which I guess isn't that long, but in some ways I feel like a forgotten man. I rarely hear from anyone, even Jan's closest friends, unless I call them. I don't understand why they haven't called or come over to see her things. Everyone is gracious when I call, but I'm like an afterthought, it seems like. I don't have anyone to talk everything out like I did with Jan—I do meet with Tony each week, but he's got his physical problems too. Once in a while I get invited over to someone's home, but it's rare, and I feel they must feel obligated to do that. I end up feeling like an inconvenient obligation. I'm someone everyone thinks about once in a while and then, "Oh yeah, let's invite him over."

Counselor: You're feeling what many fear when they're in grief—forgotten—when you want to be remembered.

Jim: That's it. And next month are four major dates that are full of hurt—the diagnosis, hospitalization . . . I wish others would remember and reach out. But they're busy with their lives. They're going on and I'm standing still.

Counselor: Unfortunately, people do forget so soon, partly because of our culture as well as churches don't teach them what to do. What could you do at this time to let others know you need them?

Jim: I'm not sure.

Counselor: One suggestion to consider is sending an email or letter to your friends letting them know about these four dates and the upcoming first anniversary and the fact that you'd like to hear more from them. Unfortunately, there are times when in the midst of our own grief we have to give others a wake-up call.

Jim: It's a possibility. I guess there's more I can do to have people around. I just don't want to be a drain on them, but I wish they would remember me. It's true. I feel like a forgotten man and that hurts, especially at this time.

Counselor: Not only did you lose Jan, but now you're feeling another loss as people drift out of your life.

Jim: Exactly. Jan's best friend has also been a real surprise. It's like she doesn't want to face Jan's death; and if she came over she'd have to face it again. I can't share what's really going on with me with my parents. They're elderly and get upset when they hear what I say. They want me to be the way I was before Jan died, and they say I'm different. I told them I am different. I'm not the same man I was. I'm not the same son. [emphatic tone of voice]

Counselor: Your parents have lost two important people in their lives—their daughter-in-law and their son the way he was.

Jim: I'd never thought of it that way before. It's true—it really is true. [pause for about 20 seconds] I just need some others to be in my life.

Counselor: What will you do this week?

Jim: I'll continue to write, since I know I can do this. And I'll work on that email to try to get people back in my life.

Analysis

It's typical for counselees to view their progress as slow or even nonexistent. In this brief encounter the counselor helps Jim see there was some progress, validated his pain as well as what he was experiencing, identified other losses and encouraged him to move on.

―――――――― CASE STUDY ――――――――
Sarah

The counselee was in her mid-forties. She had lost her husband eight months prior due to multiple strokes. He was 51, and it was a close, strong marriage. In session six she stated that she would be returning to work the next day as a hairstylist.

Sarah: When Ted had his stroke I had the next week off, so I wasn't involved in work until a week later. I've always kept my own appointment book, and I had it with me the day before I was scheduled to resume working. I sat down to call all my clients and cancel their appointments. I got through to two of them and then closed the book. I couldn't do it. I couldn't call every one, so I had called the salon and asked them to do it for me. They did.

Counselor: It was more difficult than you imagined.

Sarah: Oh yes . . . I didn't expect that. You know that first week I was going strong and I just believed that Frank would wake up, recover and go home. But when Saturday came, it finally hit me that it wasn't going to work that way and I had to make those calls, but I couldn't do it. I just couldn't do that. I was almost immobilized. Why? I don't understand.

Counselor: Perhaps there are a couple of reasons. By calling your clients you were finally facing the fact that Frank wasn't going to be all right, that this wasn't just a bad dream from which you'd wake up, but this was reality.

Sarah: Oh yes, it was facing it head-on . . . life was never going to be the same.

Counselor: Perhaps another reason for avoiding the calls was having to tell them your new story, that Frank had a stroke and sharing that with 30 other women was a bit too much. And it was another admission that this was very serious.

Sarah: [crying] Oh, it was—it was over the top—admitting he was so serious and facing it and then telling others who could get as emotional as I was, I couldn't do it.

Counselor: So, it sounds as though you made a wise decision at that time by letting others help you and sparing you some pain.

Sarah: That's true. [pause] Well, tomorrow I go back to work after eight months.

Counselor: How are you feeling about returning?

Sarah: Well, I need to financially, and the other stylists have been great about picking up my load for me and . . .

Counselor: But how are you feeling about returning to work?

Sarah: [long pause] I'm . . . I'm afraid. [very soft]

Counselor: I'm wondering if part of your fear is having to face each client, and they'll want you to tell your story and you'll have to tell it again and again.

Sarah: [softly] That's it. I cry enough now, and I'll end up crying with each one, and I'll be a mess.

Counselor: Had you thought of another way to inform them? Have you thought about how you will inform them?

Sarah: I'm not sure—they're all interested and want to know, but it's going to be too much.

Counselor: What if you gave them a letter with details of what has happened, what you need and specifically what they could do to help. Would that be workable?

Sarah: Oh, my gosh, yes—that would be such a relief.

Counselor: Would you like us to spend some time together crafting this letter?

Sarah: Yes, definitely.

Analysis

This case shows the struggle of many in grief in which they resist admitting the seriousness of what has occurred. The word "perhaps" is used to make the responses tentative rather stating "this is the way it is." The counselee even in the midst of grief needs the freedom to make some decisions; another statement was made about her ability, her "wisdom" to build her confidence in her ability to make good decisions in the midst of choices.

When she avoided sharing her feelings about returning to work, the counselor gently brought her back to the issue, and again it was given in a tentative manner.

The explanatory letter has been an important part of helping mourners share their story in a way that doesn't devastate them and at the same time gives others some information as well as direction on how to respond.

The counselee moved back and forth from feelings to thinking, and even though she cried gently throughout the session, it ended more upon a cognitive note with her engaged in a task to give her relief in the days to come. She was also encouraged to share this letter with her fellow workers as well.

CASE STUDY

Marriage Case (or Was It?)

There may be times when you see a person or a couple for issues other than grief. But in the midst of the session an unexpected turn occurs when a major loss is presented. Notice how this counselor responded to the loss and used it to access the husband's feelings as well as his response to his wife.

The counselee responds to the emotions of the other counselee that were shared verbally and nonverbally. The initial statements and interventions quickly move the couple toward a positive interchange.

Note that the intervention of this counselor is aimed not at changing feelings, but at enabling each spouse to express himself/herself fully and to accept the other's expression of feeling in a nonjudgmental way.

The counselor's interventions enable each of them to see the other's expression of feeling as a gift.

Husband: Things have been pretty hectic this week; a lot has been going on.

Counselor: You seem low to me.

Husband: Low?

Counselor: Sad, somehow. Your posture is slouched, your expression is somewhat sad, your tone is low.

Husband: Well, I am tired. I've been busy . . .

Wife: Well, Tom died Wednesday; it was sudden. You have not said much, but I'm sure it upset you.

Husband: Oh, yes. [Aside to therapist] Tom was a good friend my age that I have known for 20 years. Also our daughter went to camp this week . . .

Counselor: [interrupting] You shifted very quickly from Tom. You must have had lots of feelings about him. Could you respond to your wife's offer to hear your feelings?

Husband: [glances at wife, then down] Well, it did hit me pretty hard. It was so sudden it made me think of my own death.

Counselor: I notice you are talking to your wife but not looking at her.

Husband: [looks up with tears in eyes] I don't know why I am doing this. I never cry.

Counselor: [to wife] Your husband is giving you a gift of his feelings and you seem very far away—what are you feeling?

Wife: I have never seen him like this. It frightens me . . .

Counselor: Could you share with him? Would you look at each other and share that? [They look at each other.]

Wife: [to husband] I have never seen you cry before. It frightens me like something bad is happening.

Husband: I don't feel bad; it feels like a relief—like I have been holding it in for a long time.

Counselor: [to wife] Could you express further with your husband what his tears mean to you? [to husband] Could you listen and hear her words as an effort on her part to understand herself and you and not as a criticism of you?

Husband: I think so.

Wife: I always want you to be strong. I guess tears mean weakness to me. Yet, I don't really feel that way. People should cry if they feel like it. My father could cry, but I did not respect him very much—I never felt I could depend on him.

Counselor: [to wife] Maybe you made a connection there where there really wasn't one.

Wife: [to husband] I never thought of that. You are dependable, you have never really let me down; I am sorry if I have kept you from expressing to me what you really feel.

Husband: I guess I thought it was weak to cry too—my father was stoic, but the strong, silent type.

Counselor: [to both] So we have a discovery, that the expression of feeling, no matter the feeling, is a strength, rather than a weakness. It is the road to understanding and contact between husband and wife. Tell me more about Tom and the grief you're experiencing.

The rest of the time was spent on the husband's response to Tom's death but in a new type of setting as compared to previous sessions. Here is the interchange that occurred toward the close of the session. Note how the *counselor* built on what transpired and structured what the couple could do the next week to process the grief.

Counselor: It appears that our session today took a different direction.

Husband: Yeah, it really did . . . it's interesting—talking about Tom and how it's impacted me, us, had quite an effect upon our marriage—who would have known this? I think my tears were for Tom but also for other hurts or rejections or losses over the years. It's like I've been on a burial detail but I didn't bury the stuff as deep as I thought.

Wife: [interrupting] I think you have a lot more to revisit as well as Tom's loss . . . and I do want to hear more.

Counselor: It sounds like you're putting some things together about your life. Keep in mind that sometimes when a person has been so vulnerable, especially in the safety of this office, there may be a tendency to pull back or retreat a bit. You may feel a bit awkward exploring this on your own. What might you do to make it feel safer for you at home to continue facing your losses and grief?

Husband: I guess I'd like to spend time thinking about my losses some more and then take my wife up on her offer to hear about them. I feel her support more at this time.

Analysis

This was session where the grief was not verbalized or identified as such, but it was present. Sometimes we have to show that we're listening with our eyes and picking up what isn't said. In a marital session, it's important to help the couple talk with each other rather than through you. The counselor also drew some conclusions for this couple and encouraged them to continue at home what occurred during the session.

Endnotes

Introduction: Shattered Dreams—The Beginning of a Journey of Grief
1. Alicia Skinner Cook and Daniel S. Dworkin, *Helping the Bereaved: Therapeutic Interventions for Children, Adolescents and Adults* (New York: Basic Books, 1992), p. 169.

Chapter 1: One Stitch at a Time
1. Used by permission of the writer.

Chapter 2: Case Studies—What Would You Say or Do?
1. Kendall Johnson, *Trauma in the Lives of Children* (Alameda, CA: Hunter House, 1998), adapted, pp. 46-47.
2. Norm Wright, *The Complete Guide to Crisis and Trauma Counseling* (Ventura, CA: Regal, 2011).
3. Debra Whiting Alexander, Ph.D., *Children Changed by Trauma* (Oakland, CA: New Harbinger Publications, 1999), pp. 25-26
4. This book is available for purchase at www.hnormanwright.com (see the resources section).
5. Kenneth J. Doka, Ph.D., ed., *Living with Grief After Sudden Loss* (HFA, Taylor and Francis, 1996), p. 57.
6. The books and GriefShare materials listed in this chapter are available from Christian Marriage Enrichment (800-875-7560) or at www.hnormanwright.com.

Chapter 3: The World of Grief
1. Gregory Floyd, *In Grief Unveiled* (Brewster, MA: Paraclee Press, 1999), pp. 116-117.
2. Gerald Sittser, *A Grief Disguised* (Grand Rapids, MI: Zondervan, 1996), p. 47.
3. Anne Morrow-Lindberg, *In Camp's Unfamiliar Quotations*, 124.
4. Therese A. Rando, *How to Go On Living When Someone You Love Dies* (New York: Bantam, 1991).
5. Joanne T. Jozefowski, *The Phoenix Phenomenon* (Northvale, NJ: Jason Aronson, Inc, 2001), p. 17.
6. Carol Staudacher, *Beyond Grief* (Oakland, CA: New Harbinger Publications, 1987), adapted, p. 47.
7. Judy Tatelbaum, *The Courage to Grieve* (New York: Perennial, 1980), p. 28.
8. Ken Gire, *The Weathering Grace of God* (Ann Arbor, MI: Servant Publications, 2001), p. 109.
9. Linda Schupp, Ph.D., *Assessing and Treating Trauma and PTSD* (Eau Claire, WI: DESI, 2004), p. 3.
10. Thomas Attig, *The Heart of Grief* (New York: Oxford University Press, 2000), p. xi.
11. Ibid., pp. xii, xvi.

Chapter 4: Models of Grief
1. Joanne Jozefowski, *The Phoenix Phenomenon: Rising from the Ashes of Grief* (Northvale, NJ: Jason Aronson, Inc, 2001), pp. 22-23.
2. Susan J. Zonnebelt-Smeenge and Robert C. DeVries, *Traveling Through Grief* (Grand Rapids, MI: Baker Publishing Group, 2006), pp. 26-27.
3. Merton P. Strommen, *The Five Cries of Grief* (Minneapolis, MN: Augsburg Press, 1996), p. 31.
4. No original source.
5. Strommen, *The Five Cries of Grief*, p. 73.
6. Michael Card, *A Sacred Sorrow: Reaching Out to God in the Lost Language of Lament* (Colorado Springs, CO: NavPress, 2005), pp. 30-31.
7. Ibid., p. 129.
8. Strommen, *The Five Cries of Grief*, adapted.
9. Bob Diets, *Life After Loss* (Tucson, AZ: Fisher Books, 1988), p. 27.
10. Thomas Attig, *The Heart of Grief* (New York: Oxford University Press, 1996), adapted, pp. 99-116.
11. Ibid., adapted, pp. 142-145.
12. Ibid., adapted, pp. 143-150.

13. Ibid., p. 50.

14. Dennis Klase, Phyllis R. Silverman and Steven L. Nickman, eds., *Continuing Bonds* (New York: Taylor & Francis, 1996), taken from the article "Basic Constraints of a Theory of adolescent Sibling Bereavement," by Nancy Hogan and Lydia DeSaints, adapted, pp. 248-249.

15. Klase, Silverman and Nickman, eds., *Continuing Bonds*, adapted, pp. 244-248.

Chapter 5: The Variations and Complications of Grief—Patterns of Grief

1. Terry L. Martin, Kenneth J. Doka, *Men Don't Cry . . . Women Do: Transcending Gender Stereotypes of Grief* (Philadelphia, PA: Brunner/Mazel, 2000), p. 35.

2. Ibid., p. 4.

3. Ibid., adapted, pp. 29-52.

4. Gary W. Reece, *Trauma, Loss and Bereavement* (Eugene, OR: Resource Publications, 1999), adapted, p. 68.

5. Pauline Boss, *Ambiguous Loss: Learning to Live with Unresolved Grief* (Cambridge, MA: Harvard University Press, 1999), #12.

6. Ibid., p. 24.

7. Joanne T. Jozefowski, *The Phoenix Phenomenon: Rising from the Ashes of Grief* (Northvale, NJ: Jason Aronson, Inc. 2001), pp. 230-231.

8. Therese Rando, *Treatment of Complicated Mourning* (Champaign, IL: Research Press, 1993), pp. 672-680.

9. Kenneth J. Doka, ed., *Disenfranchised Grief* (Champaign, IL: Research Press, 2002), p. 7.

10. Jackson P. Rainer and Freida Brown, *Crisis Counseling and Therapy* (New York: Haworth Press, 2006), pp. 105-106.

11. Glenn Schiraldi, Ph.D., *The Post-Traumatic Stress Disorder Sourcebook* (New York: McGraw Hill, 2000), p. 177.

12. Doka, ed., *Disenfranchised Grief*, pp. 162-163.

13. Ibid., adapted, pp. 158-164.

Chapter 6: Handling "Relief" in Grief

1. Jennifer Ellison, Ed.D. and Chris McGonagle, Ph.D., *Liberating Losses: When Death Brings Relief* (Cambridge, MA: Perseus Publishers, 2003), p. 50.

2. Ibid., adapted, p. 59.

3. Ibid., p. 106.

4. Ibid., p. 128.

5. Ibid., p. 152.

6. Dr. Sidney B. Simon and Suzanne Simon, *Forgiveness* (New York: Warner Books, 1991), adapted, p. 43.

7. Dr. David Stoop, Ph.D., *Making Peace with Your Father* (Ventura, CA: Regal Books, 2004), adapted, pp. 187–211.

8. Ellison and McGonagle, *Liberating Losses: When Death Brings Relief*, pp. 180-181.

Chapter 7: Types of Death— Sudden and Anticipatory

1. Thomas Attig, *How We Grieve* (New York: Oxford University Press, 1996), p. 82.

2. Ibid., adapted, pp. 75-89.

3. Dana G. Cable, "Grief in the American Culture," in *Living with Grief: Who We Are, How We Grieve,* eds. Kenneth J. Doka and Joyce D. Davidson (Philadelphia, PA: Brunner/Mazel, 1998), pp. 64-65.

4. Fiona Marshall, *Losing a Parent* (Cambridge, MA: Fisher Books, 2000), p. 45.

5. Kenneth J. Doka and Joyce D. Davidson, *Living with Grief: Who We Are, How We Grieve* (Philadelphia, PA: Brunner/Mazel, 1998), p. 149.

6. Ibid., adapted, p. 149.

7. Marshall, *Losing a Parent*, pp. 66-67.

8. Diane Hambrook and Gail Eisenberg with Herma M. Rosenthal, *A Mother Loss Workbook* (New York: Harper Perennial, 1997), pp. 97-98.

9. Ibid., p. 145.

10. Jennifer Allen, "The Long Road, An Article on Anticipatory Grief," *The American Academy of Bereavement*, p. 2.

11. Ibid.

12. Maureen P. Keeley, Ph.D. and Julie M. Yingling, Ph.D., *Final Conversations* (Acton, MA: Vander Wyk & Burnham, 2007), pp. 17-18.

13. Therese Rando, Ph.D., *Grieving: How to Go On Living When Someone You Love Dies* (Lexington, MA: Lexington Books, 1988), adapted, pp. 94-102.

14. Therese Rando, *Grief, Dying and Death* (Champaign, IL: Research Press, 1984), adapted, p. 220.

15. Ibid., adapted, pp. 199-200.

16. William Hoy, *Road to Emmaus* (Compass Press, 2008), p. 68.

17. Ibid., p. 67.

18. Ibid., p. 71.

Chapter 8: When Grief Continues—Problems in Grieving and Recovery

1. Roy W. Fairchild, *Finding Hope Again: A Pastor's Guide to Counseling Depressed Persons* (San Francisco: Harper & Row, 1980), pp. 113-114.

2. Lilly Singer, Margaret Sirot and Susan Rodd, *Beyond Loss* (New York: E. P. Sutton, 1988), pp. 82-83.

3. Therese A. Rando, *Treatment of Complicated Mourning* (Champaign, IL: Research Press, 1993), adapted, pp. 205-207.

4. Therese A. Rando, *Grief, Dying and Death: Clinical Interventions for Caregivers* (Champaign, IL: Research Press, 1984), pp. 63-64.

5. J. William Worden, *Grief Counseling and Grief Therapy* (New York: Springer Publishing, 2009), p. 163.

6. Alicia Skinner Cook and Daniel S. Dworkin, *Helping the Bereaved: Therapeutic Interventions for Children, Adolescents and Adults* (New York: Basic Books, 1992), p. 47.

Chapter 9: How to Begin the Initial Session with a Grieving Person

1. Joanne T. Jozefowski, *The Phoenix Phenomenon* (Northvale, NJ: Jason Aronson, Inc, 2001), adapted, pp. 75, 102-103, 124, 151.

2. William Hoy, *Road to Emmaus* (Compass Press, 2008).

3. Therese A Rando, *Treatment of Complicated Mourning* (Champaign, IL: Research Press, 1993), p. 415.

4. Hoy, *Road to Emmaus*, p. 62.

5. Geraldine M. Humphrey and David G. Zimpfer, *Counseling for Grief and Bereavement* (Los Angeles: Sage Publications, 2008), adapted, p. 23.

6. Ibid., p. 47.

Chapter 10: The Family in Grief

1. Gary W. Reece, *Trauma, Loss and Bereavement* (Eugene, OR: Wycf and Stock Publishers, 1999), adapted, pp. 21-22.

2. *Families Facing Death* (San Francisco: Josey-Bass Publishers, 1998), pp. 19-20.

3. Lilly Singer, Margaret Sirot and Susan Rodd, *Beyond Loss: A Practical Guide Through Grief to a Meaningful Life* (New York: E.P. Dutton, 1988), pp. 82-83, 85.

4. Monica McGoldrick and Froma Walsh, eds., *Living Beyond Loss—Death in the Family* (New York: W.W. Norton, 1991), p. 8.

5. Ibid., p. 10.

6. J. William Worden, *Grief Counseling and Grief Therapy* (New York: Springer Publishing, 2009), p. 222.

7. Ibid., adapted, pp. 231-235.

8. Singer, Sirot and Rodd, *Beyond Loss: A Practical Guide Through Grief to a Meaningful Life*, pp. 92-93.

9. McGoldrick and Walsh, *Living Beyond Loss—Death in the Family,* pp. 50-51.

10. *Marriage and Family: A Christian Journal,* vol. 11, no. 2, pp. 484-485.

11. Suggested reading and books to help children: *Fears, Doubts, Blues & Pouts,* H. Norman Wright and Gary Oliver; *It's Okay to Cry,* H. Norman Wright; and *A Kid's Journey Through Grief,* Sue Beeney and Chung. All of these books are available on hnormanwright.com or by calling 1-800-875-7560.

12. Therese A. Rando, *Grief, Death and Dying* (Champaign, IL: Research Press, 1984), adapted, pp. 340-363.

Chapter 11: Helping Grievers Move on in Life—Recovering

1. Glen W. Davidson, *Understanding Mourning* (Minneapolis, MN: Augsburg Press, 1984), pp. 78-80.

2. Helen Fitzgerald, *The Mourning Handbook* (New York: Simon & Schuster, 1994), pp. 249-250.

3. Ann Kaiser Stearns, *Coming Back* (New York: Random House, 1988), pp. 85-86.

4. Claire Cloniger, *Postcards for Those that Hurt* (Dallas, TX: Word, 1995), p. 55.

5. Raymond Mitsch and Lynn Brookside, *Grieving the Loss of Someone You Love* (Ventura, CA: Regal Books, 1993), pp. 177-178.

6. Joanne T. Jozefowski, *The Phoenix Phenomenon* (Northvale, NJ: Jason Aronson, Inc, 2001), p. 131.

7. Adapted from the material developed by Terry Irish, Community Grief Support Groups, Crescent City Church of the Nazarene, Crescent City, CA, and Doctrinal Thesis at Nazarene Theological Seminary, Kansas City, MO.

8. Doug Manning, *Don't Take My Grief Away from Me* (San Francisco: Harper & Row, 1979), pp. 121-122.

9. Joyce Rupp, *Praying Our Goodbyes* (New York: Ivy Books, 1988), pp. 7-8.

10. Ibid., pp. 20-21.

11. James A. Fogarty, *The Magical Thoughts of Grieving Children* (Amityville, NY: Baywood Publishing Co., 2000), pp. 90-91.

12. Aphrodite Matsakis, Ph.D., *Trust After Trauma* (Oakland, CA: New Harbinger, 1997), adapted, pp. 234-235.

13. Adapted from Carolyn Rose, M.A. and Deborah Moncrief, LMFT, *Press On* (1999), p. 107.

14. Adapted, original source unknown.

15. Original source unknown.

16. Dr. Bruce Perry, M.D., Ph.D., *The Boy Who Was Raised as a Dog* (New York: Basic Books, 2006), p. 197.

17. Kenneth J. Doka, ed., *Disenfranchised Grief* (Champaign, IL: Research Press, 2002), adapted, pp. 157-158.

18. J. William Worden, *Grief Counseling and Grief Therapy* (New York: Springer Publishing, 2009), adapted, pp. 111-113.

Chapter 12: Grief Coaching

1. Dr. Gary Collins, *Christian Coaching* (Nashville, TN: Thomas Nelson, 2007), p. 14.

2. Laura Whitworth, Karen Kimsey-House, Henry Kimsey-House and Phillip Sandohl, *Co-Active Coaching: New Skills for Coaching People Toward Success in Work and Life* (Mountain View, CA: Davies-Black Publishing, 1998, 2007), adapted, p. 15.

3. John C. Maxwell, *Be a People Person* (Wheaton, IL: Victor Books, 1994), pp. 134-135.

4. Tony Stoltzfus, *Leadership Coaching: The Disiclines, Heart, and Skills of a Christian Coach* (Charleston, SC: BookSurge, 2005), p. 19.

5. Whitworth, Kimsey-House, Kimsey-House and Sandohl, *Co-Active Coaching,* adapted, p. 25.

6. Collins, *Christian Coaching,* p. 23.

7. Whitworth, Kimsey-House, Kimsey-House, and Sandahl, *Co-Active Coaching,* as quoted in Dr. Gary Collins, *Christian Counseling.*

8. Tony Stoltzfus, *Coaching Questions: A Coach's Guide to Powerful Asking Skills* (Virginia Beach, VA: Pegasus, 2008), adapted, p. 43.

9. Gerard Egan, *The Skilled Helper,* as quoted in Dr. Gary Collins, *Christian Counseling.*